KT-155-786

Soups & Starters

The Essential Recipe Handbook

Publisher's Note:
Raw or semi-cooked eggs should not be consumed by babies, toddlers, pregnant women,
the elderly or those suffering from recurring illness.

This is a **STAR FIRE** book
First published in 2005

Publisher and Creative Director: Nick Wells
Project Editor: Cat Emslie
Photographers: Paul Forrester, Colin Bowling and Stephen Brayne
Home Economists & Stylists: Jaqueline Bellefontaine, Mandy Phipps,
Vicki Smallwood and Penny Stephens
Art Director: Mike Spender
Layout Design: Dave Jones
Digital Design and Production: Chris Herbert
Editorial Assistant: Chelsea Edwards
Proofreader: Dawn Laker

08 10 12 11 09

3 5 7 9 10 8 6 4 2

This edition first published 2008 by
STAR FIRE
Crabtree Hall, Crabtree Lane
Fulham, London SW6 6TY
United Kingdom

www.star-fire.co.uk

Star Fire is part of the Foundry Creative Media Co. Ltd
© 2008 The Foundry Creative Media Co. Ltd

ISBN 978-1-84786-261-7

A CIP Record for this book is available from the British Library upon request

All rights reserved. No part of this publication may be reproduced, stored in a retrieval system,
or transmitted in any form or by any means, electronic, mechanical, photocopying, recording or otherwise,
without prior permission in writing of the publisher.

Every effort has been made to contact copyright holders. We apologize in advance for any omissions and
would be pleased to insert the appropriate acknowledgement in subsequent editions of this publication.

Printed in China

Soups &
Starters

The Essential Recipe Handbook

General Editor: Gina Steer

STAR FIRE

Contents

Hygiene in the Kitchen

It is important to remember that many foods can carry some form of bacteria. In most cases, the worst it will lead to is a bout of food poisoning or gastroenteritis, although for certain people this can be serious. The risk can be reduced or eliminated, however, by good hygiene and proper cooking.

Do not buy food that is past its sell-by date and do not consume food that is past its use-by date. When buying food, use the eyes and nose. If the food looks tired, limp or a bad colour or it has a rank, acrid or simply bad smell, do not buy or eat it under any circumstances.

Dish cloths and tea towels must be washed and changed regularly. Ideally use disposable cloths and replace on a daily basis. More durable cloths should be left to soak in bleach, then washed in the washing machine at a high temperature. Keep hands, utensils and food preparation surfaces clean and do not allow pets to climb on to work surfaces. Avoid handling food if suffering from an upset stomach as bacteria can be passed on through food preparation.

Buying

Avoid bulk buying where possible, especially fresh produce. Fresh foods lose their nutritional value rapidly, so buying a little at a time minimises loss of nutrients. Check that any packaging is intact and not damaged or pierced at all. Store fresh foods in the refrigerator as soon as possible.

When buying frozen foods, ensure that they are not heavily iced on the outside and that the contents feel completely frozen. Ensure that they have been stored in the cabinet at the correct storage level and the temperature is below –18°C/–0.4°F. Pack in cool bags to transport home and place in the freezer as soon as possible after purchase.

Preparation

Take special care when preparing raw meat and fish. Separate chopping boards should be used for each, and the knife, board and your hands should be thoroughly washed before handling or preparing any other food. Good quality plastic boards are available in various designs and colours. This makes differentiating easier and the plastic has the added hygienic advantage of being washable at high temperatures in the dishwasher. If using the board for fish, first wash in cold water, then in hot to prevent odour.

When cooking, be particularly careful to keep cooked and raw food separate to avoid any contamination. It is worth washing all fruits and vegetables regardless of whether they are going to be eaten raw or lightly cooked. This rule should apply even to prewashed herbs and salads.

Do not reheat food more than once. If using a microwave, always check that the food is piping hot all the way through – in theory, the food should reach 70°C/158°F and needs to be cooked at that temperature for at least three minutes to ensure that all bacteria are killed.

All poultry must be thoroughly thawed before using. Remove the food to be thawed from the freezer and place in a shallow dish to contain the juices. Leave the food in the refrigerator until it is completely thawed. A 1.4 kg/3 lb whole chicken will take about 26–30 hours to thaw. To speed up the process, immerse the chicken in cold water, making sure that the water is changed regularly. When the joints can move freely and no ice crystals remain in the cavity, the bird is completely thawed. Once thawed, remove the wrapper and pat dry. Place the chicken in a shallow dish, cover lightly and store as close to the base of the refrigerator as possible. The chicken should be cooked as soon as possible.

Some foods can be cooked from frozen including many prepacked foods such as soups, sauces, casseroles and breads. Where applicable follow the manufacturers' instructions. Vegetables and fruits can also be cooked from frozen, but meats and fish should be thawed first. The only time food can be refrozen is when the food has been thoroughly thawed then cooked. Once the food has cooled then it can be frozen again, but it should only be stored for one month.

All poultry and game (except for duck) must be cooked thoroughly. When cooked, the juices will run clear on the thickest part of the bird – the best area to try is usually the thigh. Other meats, like minced meat and pork should be cooked right the way through. Fish should turn opaque, be firm in texture and break easily into large flakes.

Make sure leftovers are reheated until piping hot and that any sauce or soup reaches boiling point first.

Storing, Refrigerating and Freezing

Meat, poultry, fish, seafood and dairy products should all be refrigerated. The temperature of the refrigerator should be between 1–5˚C/34–41˚F, while the freezer temperature should not rise above –18˚C/–0.4˚F. To ensure the optimum temperature, avoid leaving the door open for long periods. Try not to overstock as this reduces the airflow inside and therefore the effectiveness in cooling the food within.

When refrigerating cooked food, allow it to cool down quickly and completely before refrigerating. Hot food will raise the temperature of the refrigerator and possibly affect or spoil other food stored in it.

Food should always be covered. Raw and cooked food should be stored in separate parts of the refrigerator. Cooked food should be kept on the top shelves, while raw meat, poultry and fish should be placed on the bottom to avoid drips and cross–contamination. It is recommended that eggs be refrigerated in order to maintain their freshness and shelf life.

Regularly clean, defrost and clear out the refrigerator and freezer – it is worth checking the packaging to see exactly how long each product is safe to freeze. Take care that frozen foods are not stored in the freezer for too long. Blanched vegetables can be stored for one month; beef, lamb, poultry and pork for six months and unblanched vegetables and fruits in syrup for a year. Oily fish and sausages should be stored for three months. Dairy products can last four to six months, while cakes and pastries can be kept in the freezer for three to six months.

High Risk Foods

Certain foods may carry risks to people who are considered vulnerable such as the elderly, the ill, pregnant women, babies, young infants and those suffering from a recurring illness.

There is a slight chance that some eggs carry the bacteria salmonella. Cook the eggs until both the yolk and the white are firm to eliminate this risk. Pay particular attention to dishes and products incorporating lightly cooked or raw eggs, such as hollandaise sauce, mayonnaise, mousses, soufflés, meringues, custard–based dishes, ice creams and sorbets. Certain meats and poultry also carry the potential risk of salmonella and so should be cooked thoroughly until the juices run clear and there is no pinkness left. Unpasteurised products such as milk, cheese (especially soft cheese), pâté, meat (raw and cooked) all have the potential risk of listeria and should be avoided.

When buying seafood, buy from a reputable source which has a high turnover to ensure freshness. Fish should have bright clear eyes, shiny skin and bright pink or red gills. The fish should feel stiff to the touch, with a slight smell of sea air and iodine. The flesh of fish steaks and fillets should be translucent with no signs of discolouration. Molluscs such as scallops, clams and mussels are sold fresh and are still alive. Avoid any that are open or do not close when tapped lightly. In the same way, univalves such as cockles or winkles should withdraw back into their shells when lightly prodded. When choosing cephalopods such as squid and octopus they should have a firm flesh and pleasant sea smell.

As with all fish, whether it is shellfish or seafish, care is required when freezing it. It is imperative to check whether the fish has been frozen before. If it has been frozen, then it should not be frozen again under any circumstances.

Nutrition: The Role of Essential Nutrients

A healthy and well-balanced diet is the body's primary energy source. In children, it constitutes the building blocks for future health as well as providing lots of energy. In adults, it encourages self-healing and regeneration within the body. A well-balanced diet will provide the body with all the essential nutrients it needs. This can be achieved by eating a variety of foods, demonstrated in the pyramid below.

FATS

PROTEINS

milk, yogurt   meat, fish, poultry,
and cheese   eggs, nuts and pulses

**FRUITS AND
VEGETABLES**

STARCHY CARBOHYDRATES

cereals, potatoes, bread, rice and pasta

FATS

Fats fall into two categories: saturated and unsaturated. Fats are an essential part of the diet as they are a source of energy and provide essential fatty acids and fat-soluble vitamins, but it is very important that a healthy balance is achieved. The right balance should boost the body's immunity to infection and keep muscles, nerves and arteries in good condition. Saturated fats are of animal origin and can be found in dairy produce, meat, eggs, margarines and hard white cooking fat (lard) as well as in manufactured products such as pies, biscuits and cakes. A high intake of saturated fat over many years has been proven to increase heart disease and high blood cholesterol levels and often leads to weight gain. Lowering the amount of saturated fat that we consume is very important, but this does not mean that it is good to consume lots of other types of fat.

There are two kinds of unsaturated fats: polyunsaturated and monounsaturated. Polyunsaturated fats include safflower, soybean, corn and sesame oils. The Omega-3 oils in polyunsaturated fats have been found to be beneficial to coronary health and can encourage brain growth and development. They are derived from oily fish such as salmon, mackerel, herring, pilchards and sardines. It is recommended that we should eat these types of fish at least once a week. Alternative liver oil supplements are also available. The most popular oils that are high in monounsaturates are olive oil, sunflower oil and peanut oil. Monounsaturated fats are also known to help reduce the levels of cholestrol.

PROTEINS

Composed of amino acids – proteins' building blocks – proteins perform a wide variety of essential functions for the body, including supplying energy and building and repairing tissues. Good sources of proteins are eggs, milk, yogurt, cheese, meat, fish, poultry, eggs, nuts and pulses. (See the second level of the pyramid.) Some of these foods, however, contain saturated fats. To strike a nutritional balance, eat generous amounts of vegetable protein foods such as soya, beans, lentils, peas and nuts.

MINERALS

CALCIUM Important for healthy bones and teeth, nerve transmission, muscle contraction, blood clotting and hormone function. Also promotes a healthy heart and skin, relieves aching muscles and bones, maintains the correct acid–alkaline balance and reduces menstrual cramps. Good sources are dairy products, small bones of small fish, nuts, pulses, fortified white flours, breads and green leafy vegetables.

CHROMIUM Chromium balances blood sugar levels, helps to reduce cravings, improves lifespan, helps protect DNA and is essential for heart function. Good sources are brewer's yeast, wholemeal bread, rye bread, oysters, potatoes, green peppers, butter and parsnips.

IODINE Important for the manufacture of thyroid hormones and for normal development. Good sources are seafood, seaweed, milk and dairy.

IRON As a component of haemoglobin, iron carries oxygen around the body. It is vital for normal growth and development. Good sources are liver, corned beef, red meat, fortified breakfast cereals, pulses, green leafy vegetables, egg yolk, cocoa and cocoa products.

MAGNESIUM Important for efficient functioning of metabolic enzymes and development of the skeleton. Magnesium promotes healthy muscles by helping them to relax and is therefore good for PMS. It is also important for heart muscles and the nervous system. Good sources are nuts, green vegetables, meat, cereals, milk and yogurt.

PHOSPHORUS Forms and maintains bones and teeth, builds muscle tissue, helps maintain pH of the body and aids metabolism and energy production. Phosphorus is present in almost all foods.

POTASSIUM Enables processing of nutrients; promotes healthy nerves and muscles; maintains fluid balance; helps secretion of insulin for blood sugar control; relaxes muscles; maintains heart functioning and stimulates gut movement. Good sources are fruit, vegetables, milk and bread.

SELENIUM Antioxidant properties help to protect against free radicals and carcinogens. Selenium reduces inflammation, stimulates the immune system, promotes a healthy heart and helps vitamin E's action. Necessary for the male reproductive system and for metabolism. Good sources are tuna, liver, kidney, meat, eggs, cereals, nuts and dairy products.

SODIUM Important in helping to control body fluid, preventing dehydration. Sodium is involved in muscle and nerve function and helps move nutrients into cells. All foods are good sources. Processed, pickled and salted foods are richest in sodium but should be eaten in moderation.

ZINC Important for metabolism and healing; aids ability to cope with stress; promotes a healthy nervous system and brain, especially in the growing foetus; aids bone and teeth formation and is essential for energy. Good sources are liver, meat, pulses, whole–grain cereals, nuts and oysters.

VITAMINS

VITAMIN A Important for cell growth and developmemt and for the formation of visual pigments in the eye. Vitamin A comes in two forms: retinol and beta–carotenes. Retinol is found in liver, meat and whole milk. Beta–carotene is a powerful antioxidant and is found in red and yellow fruits and vegetables such as carrots, mangoes and apricots.

VITAMIN B1 Important in releasing energy from carbohydrate-containing foods. Good sources are yeast and yeast products, bread, fortified breakfast cereals and potatoes.

VITAMIN B2 Important for metabolism of proteins, fats and carbohydrates to produce energy. Good sources are meat, yeast extracts, fortified breakfast cereals and milk and its products.

VITAMIN B3 Required for the metabolism of food into energy. Good sources are milk, fortified cereals, pulses, meat, poultry and eggs.

VITAMIN B5 Important for the metabolism of food and energy production. All foods are good sources but especially fortified breakfast cereals, whole–grain bread and dairy products.

VITAMIN B6 Important for metabolism of protein and fat. Vitamin B6 may also be involved in the regulation of sex hormones. Good sources are liver, fish, pork, soya beans and peanuts.

VITAMIN B12 Important for the production of red blood cells and DNA. It is vital for growth and the nervous system. Good sources are meat, fish, eggs, poultry and milk.

BIOTIN Important for metabolism of fatty acids. Good sources of biotin are liver, kidney, eggs and nuts.

VITAMIN C Important for healing wounds and the formation of collagen which keeps skin and bones strong. It is an important antioxidant. Good sources are fruits, especially soft summer fruits, and vegetables.

VITAMIN D Important for absorption and handling of calcium to help build bone strength. Good sources are oily fish, eggs, whole milk and milk products, margarine and of course sufficient exposure to sunlight, as vitamin D is made in the skin.

VITAMIN E Important as an antioxidant vitamin helping to protect cell membranes from damage. Good sources are vegetable oils, margarines, seeds, nuts and green vegetables.

FOLIC ACID Critical during pregnancy for the development of the brain and nerves. It is always essential for brain and nerve function and is needed for utilising protein and red blood cell formation. Good sources are whole–grain cereals, fortified cereals, green leafy vegetables, oranges and liver.

VITAMIN K Important for controlling blood clotting. Good sources are cauliflower, Brussels sprouts, lettuce, cabbage, beans, broccoli, peas, asparagus, potatoes, corn oil, tomatoes and milk.

CARBOHYDRATES

Carbohydrates are an energy source and come in two forms: starch and sugar. Starch carbohydrates are also known as complex carbohydrates and they include all cereals, potatoes, breads, rice and pasta. Eating whole–grain varieties of these foods also provides fibre. Diets high in fibre are believed to be beneficial in helping to prevent bowel cancer and keep cholesterol down. Sugar carbohydrates – also known as fast–release because they provide a quick fix of energy – include sugar and sugar-sweetened products. Other sugars are lactose (from milk) and fructose (from fruit).

Soups

Soups are so simple and yet so satisfying, everyone should have a few favourite recipes they can whip up for a warming meal on a cold winter's day or as an appetizing start to a meal. Here you will find a wide range of soups catering to all tastes, including classic Tomato & Basil, exotic Thai Shellfish and hearty Potato, Leek & Rosemary.

Mushroom & Sherry Soup

1 Preheat the oven to 180°C/350°F/Gas Mark 4. Remove the crusts from the bread and cut the bread into small cubes.

2 In a large bowl, toss the cubes of bread with the lemon rind and juice, 2 tablespoons of water and plenty of freshly ground black pepper.

3 Spread the bread cubes on to a lightly oiled, large baking tray and bake for 20 minutes until golden and crisp.

4 If the wild mushrooms are small, leave some whole. Otherwise, slice all the mushrooms thinly and reserve.

5 Heat the oil in a saucepan. Add the garlic and spring onions and cook for 1–2 minutes.

6 Add the mushrooms and cook for 3–4 minutes until they start to soften. Add the chicken stock and stir to mix.

7 Bring to the boil, then reduce the heat to a gentle simmer. Cover and cook for 10 minutes.

8 Stir in the sherry, and season to taste with a little salt and pepper. Pour into warmed bowls, sprinkle over the chives and serve immediately with the lemon croutons.

Ingredients   SERVES 4

4 slices day–old white bread
zest of $\frac{1}{2}$ lemon
1 tbsp lemon juice
salt and freshly ground black pepper
125 g/4 oz assorted wild
    mushrooms, lightly rinsed
125 g/4 oz baby button
    mushrooms, wiped
2 tsp olive oil
1 garlic clove, peeled and crushed
6 spring onions, trimmed and
    diagonally sliced
600 ml/1 pint chicken stock
4 tbsp dry sherry
1 tbsp freshly snipped chives,
    to garnish

Helpful hint

To achieve very fine shreds of lemon zest, use a zester, obtainable from all kitchen shops. Or peel the fruit thinly with a vegetable peeler, then shred with a small sharp knife. When grating fruit, use a clean, dry pastry brush to remove the rind from the grater.

2

4

6

Chinese Chicken Soup

1 Remove any skin from the chicken. Place on a chopping board and use two forks to tear the chicken into fine shreds.

2 Heat the oil in a large saucepan and fry the spring onions and chilli for 1 minute.

3 Add the garlic and ginger and cook for another minute.

4 Stir in the chicken stock and gradually bring the mixture to the boil.

5 Break up the noodles a little and add to the boiling stock with the carrot.

6 Stir to mix, then reduce the heat to a simmer and cook for 3–4 minutes.

7 Add the shredded chicken, bean sprouts, soy sauce and fish sauce and stir.

8 Cook for a further 2–3 minutes until piping hot. Ladle the soup into bowls and sprinkle with the coriander leaves. Serve immediately.

Ingredients   SERVES 4

225 g/8 oz cooked chicken
1 tsp sesame oil
6 spring onions, trimmed and
    diagonally sliced
1 red chilli, deseeded and finely
    chopped
1 garlic clove, peeled and crushed
2.5 cm/1 inch piece root ginger,
    peeled and finely grated
1 litre/1$^3/_4$ pints chicken stock
150 g/5 oz medium egg noodles
1 carrot, peeled and cut into
    matchsticks
125 g/4 oz bean sprouts
2 tbsp soy sauce
1 tbsp fish sauce
fresh coriander leaves, to garnish

Tasty tip

For added nutritional value, substitute the egg noodles with the wholewheat variety. Increase the vegetable content by adding 75 g/3 oz each of water chestnuts and bamboo shoots and 50 g/2 oz of sugar snap peas and baby corn in step 7.

Carrot & Ginger Soup

1   Preheat the oven to 180°C/350°F/Gas Mark 4. Roughly chop the bread. Dissolve the yeast extract in 2 tablespoons of warm water and mix with the bread.

2   Spread the bread cubes over a lightly oiled baking tray and bake for 20 minutes, turning halfway through. Remove from the oven and reserve.

3   Heat the oil in a large saucepan. Gently cook the onion and garlic for 3–4 minutes.

4   Stir in the ground ginger and cook for 1 minute to release the flavour.

5   Add the chopped carrots, then stir in the stock and the fresh ginger. Simmer gently for 15 minutes.

6   Remove from the heat and allow to cool a little. Blend until smooth, then season to taste with salt and pepper. Stir in the lemon juice. Garnish with the chives and lemon zest and serve immediately.

Ingredients   SERVES 4

4 slices bread, crusts removed
1 tsp yeast extract
2 tsp olive oil
1 onion, peeled and chopped
1 garlic clove, peeled and crushed
$^1/_2$ tsp ground ginger
450 g/1 lb carrots, peeled and
   chopped
1 litre/1$^3/_4$ pints vegetable stock
2.5 cm/1 inch piece root ginger,
   peeled and finely grated
salt and freshly ground black pepper
1 tbsp lemon juice

To garnish:
chives
lemon zest

Tasty tip
For special occasions, serve with a spoonful of lightly whipped cream or créme fraîche.

Italian Bean Soup

1   Heat the oil in a large saucepan. Add the leek, garlic and
    oregano and cook gently for 5 minutes, stirring occasionally.

2   Stir in the green beans and the cannellini beans. Sprinkle in
    the pasta and pour in the stock.

3   Bring the stock mixture to the boil, then reduce the heat
    to a simmer.

4   Cook for 12–15 minutes or until the vegetables are tender
    and the pasta is cooked to 'al dente'. Stir occasionally.

5   In a heavy-based frying pan, dry-fry the tomatoes over a
    high heat until they soften and the skins begin to blacken.

6   Gently crush the tomatoes in the pan with the back of a
    spoon and add to the soup.

7   Season to taste with salt and pepper. Stir in the shredded
    basil and serve immediately.

Ingredients   SERVES 4

2 tsp olive oil
1 leek, washed and chopped
1 garlic clove, peeled and crushed
2 tsp dried oregano
75 g/3 oz green beans, trimmed and
    cut into bite-size pieces
410 g can cannellini beans, drained
    and rinsed
75 g/3 oz small pasta shapes
1 litre/1$^3/_4$ pints vegetable stock
8 cherry tomatoes

Tasty tip

This soup tastes even better the day
after it has been made. Make the
soup the day before you intend
serving it and add a little extra stock
when reheating.

Tomato & Basil Soup

1 Preheat the oven to 200°C/400°F/Gas Mark 6. Evenly spread the tomatoes and unpeeled garlic in a single layer in a large roasting tin.

2 Mix the oil and vinegar together. Drizzle over the tomatoes and sprinkle with the dark brown sugar.

3 Roast the tomatoes in the preheated oven for 20 minutes until tender and lightly charred in places.

4 Remove from the oven and allow to cool slightly. When cool enough to handle, squeeze the softened flesh of the garlic from the papery skin. Place with the charred tomatoes in a nylon sieve over a saucepan.

5 Press the garlic and tomato through the sieve with the back of a wooden spoon.

6 When all the flesh has been sieved, add the tomato purée and vegetable stock to the pan. Heat gently, stirring occasionally.

7 In a small bowl, beat the yogurt and basil together and season to taste with salt and pepper. Stir the basil yogurt into the soup. Garnish with basil leaves and serve immediately.

Ingredients SERVES 4

1.1 kg/2¹/₂ lb ripe tomatoes,
 cut in half
2 garlic cloves
1 tsp olive oil
1 tbsp balsamic vinegar
1 tbsp dark brown sugar
1 tbsp tomato purée
300 ml/¹/₂ pint vegetable stock
6 tbsp natural yogurt
2 tbsp freshly chopped basil
salt and freshly ground black pepper
small basil leaves, to garnish

Tasty tip

Use the sweetest type of tomatoes available as it makes a big difference to the flavour of the soup. Many supermarkets now stock speciality ranges grown slowly and matured for longer on the vine to give them an intense flavour. If these are unavailable, add a little extra sugar to bring out the flavour.

Prawn & Chilli Soup

1 To make spring onion curls, finely shred the spring onions lengthways. Place in a bowl of ice–cold water and reserve.

2 Remove the heads and shells from the prawns, leaving the tails intact.

3 Split the prawns almost in two to form a butterfly shape and individually remove the black thread that runs down the back of each one.

4 In a large pan, heat the stock with the lime rind and juice, fish sauce, chilli and soy sauce.

5 Bruise the lemon grass by crushing it along its length with a rolling pin, then add to the stock mixture.

6 When the stock mixture is boiling, add the prawns and cook until they are pink.

7 Remove the lemon grass and add the rice vinegar and coriander.

8 Ladle into bowls and garnish with the spring onion curls. Serve immediately.

Ingredients   SERVES 4

2 spring onions, trimmed
225 g/8 oz whole raw tiger prawns
750 ml/1¼ pints fish stock
juice and finely grated rind of 1 lime
1 tbsp fish sauce
1 red chilli, deseeded and chopped
1 tbsp soy sauce
1 lemon grass stalk
2 tbsp rice vinegar
4 tbsp freshly chopped coriander

Tasty tip

For a more substantial dish, cook 50–75 g/2–3 oz Thai fragrant rice for 12–15 minutes, or until just cooked. Drain, then place a little in the soup bowl and ladle the prepared soup on top.

Curried Parsnip Soup

1 In a small frying pan, dry–fry the cumin and coriander seeds over a moderately high heat for 1–2 minutes. Shake the pan during cooking until the seeds are lightly toasted.

2 Reserve until cooled. Grind the toasted seeds in a pestle and mortar.

3 Heat the oil in a saucepan. Cook the onion until softened and starting to turn golden.

4 Add the garlic, turmeric, chilli powder and cinnamon stick to the pan. Continue to cook for a further minute.

5 Add the parsnips and stir well. Pour in the stock and bring to the boil. Cover and simmer for 15 minutes or until the parsnips are cooked.

6 Allow the soup to cool. Once cooled, remove the cinnamon stick and discard.

7 Blend the soup in a food processor until very smooth.

8 Transfer to a saucepan and reheat gently. Season to taste with salt and pepper. Garnish with fresh coriander and serve immediately with the yogurt.

Ingredients   SERVES 4

1 tsp cumin seeds
2 tsp coriander seeds
1 tsp oil
1 onion, peeled and chopped
1 garlic clove, peeled and crushed
$1/_2$ tsp turmeric
$1/_4$ tsp chilli powder
1 cinnamon stick
450 g/1 lb parsnips, peeled and
    chopped
1 litre/$1^3/_4$ pints vegetable stock
salt and freshly ground black pepper
2–3 tbsp natural yogurt, to serve
fresh coriander leaves, to garnish

Food Fact

Parsnips vary in colour from pale yellow to a creamy white. They are at their best when they are the size of a large carrot. If larger, remove the central core which can be woody.

Roasted Red Pepper, Tomato & Red Onion Soup

1 Preheat the oven to 190°C/375°F/Gas Mark 5. Pour the oil into a large roasting tin and place the peppers and onion in the base, tossing to coat. Cook in the oven for 10 minutes. Add the tomatoes and cook for a further 20 minutes or until the peppers are soft.

2 Cut the bread into 1 cm/^{1}/$_2$ inch slices. Cut the garlic clove in half and rub the cut edge of the garlic over the bread.

3 Place all the bread slices on a large baking tray, and bake in the preheated oven for 10 minutes, turning halfway through, until golden and crisp.

4 Remove the vegetables from the oven and allow to cool slightly, then blend in a food processor until smooth. Strain the vegetable mixture through a large nylon sieve into a saucepan, to remove the seeds and skin. Add the stock, season to taste with salt and pepper and stir to mix. Heat the soup gently until piping hot.

5 In a small bowl, beat together the Worcestershire sauce with the fromage frais.

6 Pour the soup into warmed bowls and swirl a spoonful of the fromage frais mixture into each bowl. Serve immediately with the garlic toasts.

Ingredients SERVES 4

2 tsp olive oil

2 large red peppers, deseeded and roughly chopped

1 red onion, peeled and roughly chopped

350 g/12 oz tomatoes, halved

1 small crusty French loaf

1 garlic clove, peeled

600 ml/1 pint vegetable stock

salt and freshly ground black pepper

1 tsp Worcestershire sauce

4 tbsp fromage frais

Helpful hint

A quick, hassle–free way to remove the skin from peppers once they have been roasted or grilled is to place them in a polythene bag. Leave for 10 minutes or until cool enough to handle, then simply peel the skin away from the flesh.

Swede, Turnip, Parsnip & Potato Soup

1 Finely chop 1 onion. Melt the butter in a large saucepan and add the onion, carrots, swede, turnip, parsnip and potatoes. Cover and cook gently for about 10 minutes, without colouring. Stir occasionally during this time.

2 Add the stock and season to taste with the nutmeg, salt and pepper. Cover and bring to the boil, then reduce the heat and simmer gently for 15–20 minutes, or until the vegetables are tender. Remove from the heat and leave to cool for 30 minutes.

3 Heat the oil in a large heavy–based frying pan. Add the onions and cook over a medium heat for about 2–3 minutes, stirring frequently, until golden brown. Remove the onions with a slotted spoon and drain well on absorbent kitchen paper. As they cool, they will turn crispy.

4 Pour the cooled soup into a food processor or blender and process to form a smooth purée. Return to the pan, adjust the seasoning, then stir in the cream. Gently reheat and top with the crispy onions. Serve immediately with chunks of bread.

Ingredients   SERVES 4

2 large onions, peeled
25 g/1 oz butter
2 medium carrots, peeled and
    roughly chopped
175 g/6 oz swede, peeled and
    roughly chopped
125 g/4 oz turnip, peeled and
    roughly chopped
125 g/4 oz parsnips, peeled and
    roughly chopped
175 g/6 oz potatoes, peeled
1 litre/1³/₄ pints vegetable stock
¹/₂ tsp freshly grated nutmeg
salt and freshly ground black pepper
4 tbsp vegetable oil, for frying
125 ml/4 fl oz double cream
warm crusty bread, to serve

Helpful hint

For a lower–fat version of this delicious soup, add milk (skimmed if preferred) rather than cream when reheating.

Potato & Fennel Soup

1   Melt the butter in a large heavy–based saucepan. Add the onions with the garlic and half the salt, and cook over a medium heat, stirring occasionally, for 7–10 minutes, or until the onions are very soft and beginning to turn brown.

2   Add the potatoes, fennel bulb, caraway seeds and the remaining salt. Cook for about 5 minutes, then pour in the vegetable stock. Bring to the boil, partially cover and simmer for 15–20 minutes, or until the potatoes are tender. Stir in the chopped parsley and adjust the seasoning to taste.

3   For a smooth–textured soup, allow to cool slightly then pour into a food processor or blender and blend until smooth. Reheat the soup gently, then ladle into individual soup bowls. For a chunky soup, omit this blending stage and ladle straight from the saucepan into soup bowls.

4   Swirl a spoonful of crème fraîche into each bowl and serve immediately with roughly–torn pieces of French stick.

Ingredients   SERVES 4

25 g/1 oz butter
2 large onions, peeled and thinly
   sliced
2–3 garlic cloves, peeled and crushed
1 tsp salt
2 medium potatoes (about 450 g/1
   lb in weight), peeled and diced
1 fennel bulb, trimmed and finely
   chopped
$^1/_2$ tsp caraway seeds
1 litre/1$^3/_4$ pints vegetable stock
freshly ground black pepper
2 tbsp freshly chopped parsley
4 tbsp crème fraîche
roughly torn pieces of French stick,
   to serve

Food fact

A fennel bulb is the swollen stem of a plant known as Florence fennel. Originating in Italy, Florence fennel has a distinct aniseed flavour, which mellows and sweetens when cooked. Look out for well–rounded bulbs with bright green fronds.

Cawl

1 Put the lamb in a large saucepan, cover with cold water and bring to the boil. Add a generous pinch of salt. Simmer gently for 1¹/₂ hours, then set aside to cool completely, preferably overnight.

2 The next day, skim the fat off the surface of the lamb liquid and discard. Return the saucepan to the heat and bring back to the boil. Simmer for 5 minutes. Add the onions, potatoes, parsnips, swede and carrots and return to the boil. Reduce the heat, cover and cook for about 20 minutes, stirring occasionally.

3 Add the leeks and season to taste with salt and pepper. Cook for a further 10 minutes, or until all the vegetables are tender.

4 Using a slotted spoon, remove the meat from the saucepan and take the meat off the bone. Discard the bones and any gristle, then return the meat to the pan. Adjust the seasoning to taste, stir in the parsley, then serve immediately with plenty of warm crusty bread.

Ingredients   SERVES 4–6

700 g/1¹/₂ lb scrag end of lamb or
   best end of neck chops
pinch of salt
2 large onions, peeled and
   thinly sliced
3 large potatoes, peeled and cut
   into chunks
2 parsnips, peeled and cut
   into chunks
1 swede, peeled and cut into chunks
3 large carrots, peeled and cut
   into chunks
2 leeks, trimmed and sliced
freshly ground black pepper
4 tbsp freshly chopped parsley
warm crusty bread, to serve

Food fact

Many traditional Welsh recipes such as Cawl feature lamb. This flavoursome soup was once a staple dish, originally made with scraps of mutton or lamb and vegetables cooked together in a broth. Use Welsh lamb if possible for this modern version, as the meat is lean and tender.

Potato, Leek & Rosemary Soup

1 Melt the butter in a large saucepan, add the leeks and cook gently for 5 minutes, stirring frequently. Remove 1 tablespoon of the cooked leeks and reserve for garnishing.

2 Add the potatoes, vegetable stock, rosemary sprigs and milk. Bring to the boil, then reduce the heat, cover and simmer gently for 20–25 minutes, or until the vegetables are tender.

3 Cool for 10 minutes. Discard the rosemary, then pour into a food processor or blender and blend well to form a smooth-textured soup.

4 Return the soup to the saucepan and stir in the chopped parsley and crème fraîche. Season to taste with salt and pepper. If the soup is too thick, stir in a little more milk or water. Reheat gently without boiling, then ladle into warm soup bowls. Garnish the soup with the reserved leeks and serve immediately with wholemeal rolls.

Ingredients   SERVES 4

50 g/2 oz butter
450 g/1 lb leeks, trimmed and
    finely sliced
700 g/1$^1/_2$ lb potatoes, peeled and
    roughly chopped
900 ml/1$^1/_2$ pints vegetable stock
4 sprigs of fresh rosemary
450 ml/$^3/_4$ pint full-cream milk
2 tbsp freshly chopped parsley
2 tbsp crème fraîche
salt and freshly ground black pepper
wholemeal rolls, to serve

Tasty tip

This rosemary-scented version of vichyssoise is equally delicious served cold. Allow the soup to cool before covering, then chill in the refrigerator for at least 2 hours. The soup will thicken as it chills, so you may need to thin it to the desired consistency with more milk or stock and season before serving. It is important to use fresh rosemary rather than dried for this recipe.

Cream of Spinach Soup

1 Place the onion, garlic and potatoes in a large saucepan and cover with the cold water. Add half the salt and bring to the boil. Cover and simmer for 15–20 minutes, or until the potatoes are tender. Remove from the heat and add the spinach. Cover and set aside for 10 minutes.

2 Slowly melt the butter in another saucepan, add the flour and cook over a low heat for about 2 minutes. Remove the saucepan from the heat and add the milk, a little at a time, stirring continuously. Return to the heat and cook, stirring continuously, for 5–8 minutes, or until the sauce is smooth and slightly thickened. Add the freshly grated nutmeg to taste.

3 Blend the cooled potato and spinach mixture in a food processor or blender to a smooth purée, then return to the saucepan and gradually stir in the white sauce. Season to taste with salt and pepper and gently reheat, taking care not to allow the soup to boil. Ladle into soup bowls and top with spoonfuls of crème fraîche or soured cream. Serve immediately with warm foccacia bread.

Ingredients   SERVES 6–8

1 large onion, peeled and chopped
5 large plump garlic cloves, peeled and chopped
2 medium potatoes, peeled and chopped
750 ml/1¼ pints cold water
1 tsp salt
450 g/1 lb spinach, washed and large stems removed
50 g/2 oz butter
3 tbsp flour
750 ml/1¼ pints milk
½ tsp freshly grated nutmeg
freshly ground black pepper
6–8 tbsp crème fraîche or soured cream
warm foccacia bread, to serve

Helpful hint

When choosing spinach, always look for fresh, crisp, dark green leaves. Use within 1–2 days of buying and store in a cool place. To prepare, wash in several changes of water to remove any dirt or grit and shake off as much excess water as possible.

Rice & Tomato Soup

1 Preheat the oven to 220°C/425°F/Gas Mark 7. Rinse and drain the basmati rice. Place the canned tomatoes with their juice in a large heavy-based saucepan with the garlic, lime rind, oil and sugar. Season to taste with salt and pepper. Bring to the boil, then reduce the heat, cover and simmer for 10 minutes.

2 Add the boiling vegetable stock or water and the rice, then cook, uncovered, for a further 15–20 minutes, or until the rice is tender. If the soup is too thick, add a little more water. Reserve and keep warm, if the croutons are not ready.

3 Meanwhile, to make the croutons, mix the pesto and olive oil in a large bowl. Add the bread cubes and toss until they are coated completely with the mixture. Spread on a baking sheet and bake in the preheated oven for 10–15 minutes, until golden and crisp, turning them over halfway through cooking. Serve the soup immediately sprinkled with the warm croutons.

Ingredients   SERVES 4

150 g/5 oz easy-cook basmati rice
400 g can chopped tomatoes
2 garlic cloves, peeled and crushed
grated rind of ¹/₂ lime
2 tbsp extra virgin olive oil
1 tsp sugar
salt and freshly ground pepper
300 ml/¹/₂ pint vegetable stock
   or water

For the croutons:

2 tbsp prepared pesto sauce
2 tbsp olive oil
6 thin slices ciabatta bread, cut into
   1 cm/¹/₂ inch cubes

Helpful hint

Pesto is a vivid green sauce, made from basil leaves, garlic, pine nuts, Parmesan cheese and olive oil. Shop-bought pesto is fine for this quick soup, but try making your own during the summer when basil is plentiful.

Coconut Chicken Soup

1 Discard the outer leaves of the lemon grass stalks, then place on a chopping board and, using a mallet or rolling pin, pound gently to bruise; reserve.

2 Heat the vegetable oil in a large saucepan and cook the onions over a medium heat for about 10–15 minutes until soft and beginning to change colour.

3 Lower the heat, stir in the garlic, ginger, lime leaves and turmeric and cook for 1 minute. Add the red pepper, coconut milk, stock, lemon grass and rice. Bring to the boil, cover and simmer gently over a low heat for about 10 minutes.

4 Cut the chicken into bite-size pieces, then stir into the soup with the sweetcorn and the freshly chopped coriander. Add the Thai fish sauce, or a few dashes to taste, then reheat gently, stirring frequently. Serve immediately with a few chopped pickled chillies to sprinkle on top.

Ingredients   SERVES 4

2 lemon grass stalks
3 tbsp vegetable oil
3 medium onions, peeled and
  finely sliced
3 garlic cloves, peeled and crushed
2 tbsp fresh root ginger, finely grated
2–3 kaffir lime leaves
$1\frac{1}{2}$ tsp turmeric
1 red pepper, deseeded and diced
400 ml can coconut milk
1.1 litres/2 pints vegetable or
  chicken stock
275 g/9 oz easy–cook long–grain
  rice
275 g/10 oz cooked chicken meat
285 g can sweetcorn, drained
3 tbsp freshly chopped coriander
1 tbsp Thai fish sauce
freshly chopped pickled chillies,
  to serve

Hot-&-Sour Mushroom Soup

1 Heat the oil in a frying pan, add the garlic and shallots and cook until golden brown and starting to crisp. Remove from the pan and reserve. Add the chillies to the pan and cook until they start to change colour.

2 Place the garlic, shallots and chillies in a food processor or blender and blend to a smooth purée with 150 ml/¼ pint water. Pour the purée back into the pan, add the sugar with a large pinch of salt, then cook gently, stirring, until dark in colour. Take care not to burn the mixture.

3 Pour the stock into a large saucepan, add the garlic purée, rice, lime leaves, soy sauce and the lemon rind and juice. Bring to the boil, then reduce the heat, cover and simmer gently for about 10 minutes.

4 Add the mushrooms and simmer for a further 10 minutes, or until the mushrooms and rice are tender. Remove the lime leaves, stir in the chopped coriander and ladle into bowls. Place the chopped green chillies and spring onions in small bowls and serve separately to sprinkle on top of the soup.

Ingredients   SERVES 4

4 tbsp sunflower oil
3 garlic cloves, peeled and
    finely chopped
3 shallots, peeled and finely chopped
2 large red chillies, deseeded and
    finely chopped
1 tbsp soft brown sugar
large pinch of salt
1 litre/1¾ pints vegetable stock
250 g/9 oz Thai fragrant rice
5 kaffir lime leaves, torn
2 tbsp soy sauce
juice and grated rind of 1 lemon
250 g/9 oz oyster mushrooms, wiped
    and cut into pieces
2 tbsp freshly chopped coriander

To garnish:

2 green chillies, deseeded and
    finely chopped
3 spring onions, trimmed and
    finely chopped

Bacon & Split Pea Soup

1 Cover the dried split peas with plenty of cold water, cover loosely and leave to soak for a minimum of 12 hours, preferably overnight.

2 Melt the butter in a heavy–based saucepan, add the garlic and onion and cook for 2–3 minutes, without colouring. Add the rice, drained split peas and tomato purée and cook for 2–3 minutes, stirring constantly to prevent sticking. Add the stock, bring to the boil, then reduce the heat and simmer for 20–25 minutes, or until the rice and peas are tender. Remove from the heat and leave to cool.

3 Blend about three–quarters of the soup in a food processor or blender to form a smooth purée. Pour the purée into the remaining soup in the saucepan. Add the carrots to the saucepan and cook for a further 10–12 minutes, or until the carrots are tender.

4 Meanwhile, place the bacon in a non–stick frying pan and cook over a gentle heat until the bacon is crisp. Remove and drain on absorbent kitchen paper.

5 Season the soup with salt and pepper to taste, then stir in the parsley and cream. Reheat for 2–3 minutes, then ladle into soup bowls. Sprinkle with the bacon and serve immediately with warm garlic bread.

Ingredients   SERVES 4

50 g/2 oz dried split peas
25 g/1 oz butter
1 garlic clove, peeled and
 finely chopped
1 medium onion, peeled and thinly
 sliced
175 g/6 oz long–grain rice
2 tbsp tomato purée
1.1 litres/2 pints vegetable or
 chicken stock
175 g/6 oz carrots, peeled and
 finely diced
125 g/4 oz streaky bacon,
 finely chopped
salt and freshly ground black pepper
2 tbsp freshly chopped parsley
4 tbsp single cream
warm crusty garlic bread, to serve

Pumpkin & Smoked Haddock Soup

1   Heat the oil in a large heavy–based saucepan and gently cook the onion, garlic, and celery for about 10 minutes. This will release the sweetness but not colour the vegetables. Add the pumpkin and potatoes to the saucepan and stir to coat the vegetables with the oil.

2   Gradually pour in the stock and bring to the boil. Cover, then reduce the heat and simmer for 25 minutes, stirring occasionally. Stir in the dry sherry, then remove the saucepan from the heat and leave to cool for 5–10 minutes.

3   Blend the mixture in a food processor or blender to form a chunky purée and return to the saucepan.

4   Meanwhile, place the fish in a shallow frying pan. Pour in the milk with 3 tablespoons of water and bring to almost boiling point. Reduce the heat, cover and simmer for 6 minutes, or until the fish is cooked and flakes easily. Remove from the heat and, using a slotted spoon, remove the fish from the liquid, reserving both liquid and fish.

5   Discard the skin and any bones from the fish and flake into pieces. Stir the fish liquid into the soup, together with the flaked fish. Season with freshly ground black pepper, stir in the parsley and serve immediately.

Ingredients   SERVES 4–6

2 tbsp olive oil
1 medium onion, peeled
   and chopped
2 garlic cloves, peeled and chopped
3 celery stalks, trimmed and chopped
700 g/1¼ lb pumpkin, peeled,
   deseeded and cut into chunks
450 g/1 lb potatoes, peeled and cut
   into chunks
750 ml/1¼ pints chicken
   stock, heated
125 ml/4 fl oz dry sherry
200 g/7 oz smoked haddock fillet
150 ml/¼ pint milk
freshly ground black pepper
2 tbsp freshly chopped parsley

Tasty tip

Try to find undyed smoked haddock for this soup rather than the brightly coloured yellow type, as the texture and flavour is better.

Clear Chicken & Mushroom Soup

1 Skin the chicken legs and remove any fat. Cut each in half to make two thigh and two drumstick portions and reserve. Heat the groundnut and sesame oils in a large saucepan. Add the sliced onion and cook gently for 10 minutes, or until soft but not beginning to colour.

2 Add the chopped ginger to the saucepan and cook for about 30 seconds, stirring all the time to prevent it sticking, then pour in the stock. Add the chicken pieces and the lemon grass, cover and simmer gently for 15 minutes. Stir in the rice and cook for a further 15 minutes or until the chicken is cooked.

3 Remove the chicken from the saucepan and leave until cool enough to handle. Finely shred the flesh, then return to the saucepan with the mushrooms, spring onions, soy sauce and sherry. Simmer for 5 minutes, or until the rice and mushrooms are tender. Remove the lemon grass.

4 Season the soup to taste with salt and pepper. Ladle into warmed serving bowls, making sure each has an equal amount of shredded chicken and vegetables and serve immediately.

Ingredients   SERVES 4

2 large chicken legs, about 450 g/1 lb
    total weight
1 tbsp groundnut oil
1 tsp sesame oil
1 onion, peeled and very thinly sliced
2.5 cm/1 inch piece root ginger,
    peeled and very finely chopped
1.1 litres/2 pints clear chicken stock
1 lemon grass stalk, bruised
50 g/2 oz long–grain rice
75 g/3 oz button mushrooms, wiped
    and finely sliced
4 spring onions, trimmed, cut into
    5 cm/2 inch pieces and shredded
1 tbsp dark soy sauce
4 tbsp dry sherry
salt and freshly ground black pepper

Food fact

Tahini is a thick paste made from sesame seeds. It is available from many delicatessens and supermarkets as well as Oriental food stores. It is most often used in making houmous.

Creamy Chicken & Tofu Soup

1 Cut the tofu into 1 cm/¹/₂ inch cubes, then pat dry on absorbent kitchen paper.

2 Heat 1 tablespoon of the oil in a non-stick frying pan. Fry the tofu in two batches for 3–4 minutes or until golden brown. Remove, drain on absorbent kitchen paper and reserve.

3 Heat the remaining oil in a large saucepan. Add the garlic, ginger, galangal and lemon grass and cook for about 30 seconds. Stir in the turmeric, then pour in the stock and coconut milk and bring to the boil. Reduce the heat to a gentle simmer, add the cauliflower and carrots and simmer for 10 minutes. Add the green beans and simmer for a further 5 minutes.

4 Meanwhile, bring a large saucepan of lightly salted water to the boil. Add the noodles, turn off the heat, cover and leave to cook or cook according to the packet instructions.

5 Remove the lemon grass from the soup. Drain the noodles and stir into the soup with the chicken and browned tofu. Season to taste with salt and pepper, then simmer gently for 2–3 minutes or until heated through. Serve immediately in warmed soup bowls.

Ingredients   SERVES 4–6

225 g/8 oz firm tofu, drained
3 tbsp groundnut oil
1 garlic clove, peeled and crushed
2.5 cm/1 inch piece root ginger, peeled and finely chopped
2.5 cm/1 inch piece fresh galangal, peeled and finely sliced (if available)
1 lemon grass stalk, bruised
¹/₄ tsp ground turmeric
600 ml/1 pint chicken stock
600 ml/1 pint coconut milk
225 g/8 oz cauliflower, cut into tiny florets
1 medium carrot, peeled and cut into thin matchsticks
125 g/4 oz green beans, trimmed and cut in half
75 g/3 oz thin egg noodles
225 g/8 oz cooked chicken, shredded
salt and freshly ground black pepper

Food fact

Tofu is a white curd made from soya beans. It originated in China and is made in a similar way to cheese.

1

2

3

Wonton Noodle Soup

1   Place the mushrooms in a bowl, cover with warm water and leave to soak for 1 hour. Drain, remove and discard the stalks and finely chop the mushrooms. Return to the bowl with the prawns, pork, water chestnuts, 2 of the spring onions and egg white. Season to taste with salt and pepper. Mix well.

2   Mix the cornflour with 1 tablespoon of cold water to make a paste. Place a wonton wrapper on a board and brush the edges with the paste. Drop a little less than 1 teaspoon of the pork mixture in the centre then fold in half to make a triangle, pressing the edges together. Bring the two outer corners together, fixing together with a little more paste. Continue until all the pork mixture is used up; you should have 16–20 wontons.

3   Pour the stock into a large, wide saucepan, add the ginger slices and bring to the boil. Add the wontons and simmer for about 5 minutes. Add the noodles and cook for 1 minute. Stir in the pak choi and cook for a further 2 minutes, or until the noodles and pak choi are tender and the wontons have floated to the surface and are cooked through.

4   Ladle the soup into warmed bowls, discarding the ginger. Sprinkle with the remaining sliced spring onion and serve immediately.

Ingredients   SERVES 4

4 shiitake mushrooms, wiped
125 g/4 oz raw prawns, peeled and
   finely chopped
125 g/4 oz pork mince
4 water chestnuts, finely chopped
4 spring onions, trimmed and
   finely sliced
1 medium egg white
salt and freshly ground black pepper
1½ tsp cornflour
1 packet fresh wonton wrappers
1.1 litres/2 pints chicken stock
2 cm/¾ inch piece root ginger,
   peeled and sliced
75 g/3 oz thin egg noodles
125 g/4 oz pak choi, shredded

Food fact

Wonton wrappers are thin, almost see–through sheets of dough made from eggs and flour, about 10 cm/4 inches square. Buy them fresh or frozen from larger supermarkets and Asian stores.

Thai Shellfish Soup

1 Peel the prawns. Using a sharp knife, remove the black vein along the back of the prawns. Pat dry with absorbent kitchen paper and reserve.

2 Skin the fish, pat dry and cut into 2.5 cm/1 inch chunks. Place in a bowl with the prawns and the squid rings. Sprinkle with the lime juice and reserve.

3 Scrub the mussels, removing their beards and any barnacles. Discard any mussels that are open, damaged or that do not close when tapped. Place in a large saucepan and add 150 ml/¼ pint of coconut milk. Cover, bring to the boil, then simmer for 5 minutes, or until the mussels open, shaking the saucepan occasionally. Lift out the mussels, discarding any unopened ones, strain the liquid through a muslin-lined sieve and reserve.

4 Rinse and dry the saucepan. Heat the groundnut oil, add the curry paste and cook for 1 minute, stirring all the time. Add the lemon grass, lime leaves and fish sauce and pour in both the strained and the remaining coconut milk. Bring to a very gentle simmer. Add the fish mixture to the saucepan and simmer for 2–3 minutes or until just cooked. Stir in the mussels, with or without their shells, as preferred. Season to taste with salt and pepper, then garnish with coriander leaves. Ladle into warmed bowls and serve immediately.

Ingredients   SERVES 4–6

350 g/12 oz raw prawns
350 g/12 oz firm white fish, such as
    monkfish, cod or haddock
175 g/6 oz small squid rings
1 tbsp lime juice
450 g/1 lb live mussels
400 ml/15 fl oz coconut milk
1 tbsp groundnut oil
2 tbsp Thai red curry paste
1 lemon grass stalk, bruised
3 kaffir lime leaves, finely shredded
2 tbsp Thai fish sauce
salt and freshly ground black pepper
fresh coriander leaves, to garnish

Food fact

Sprinkling fish and seafood with lime juice improves its texture, as the acid in the juice firms up the flesh.

Wonton Soup

1 Chop the chicken into 6–8 pieces and put into a large stock pot or saucepan of water with the remaining stock ingredients. Place over a high heat and bring to the boil, skimming off any scum which rises to the surface. Reduce the heat and simmer for 2–3 hours, skimming occasionally.

2 Strain the stock through a fine sieve into a large bowl. Leave to cool, then chill in the refrigerator for 5–6 hours, or overnight. When cold, skim off the fat and remove any remaining small pieces of fat by dragging a piece of absorbent kitchen paper lightly across the surface.

3 Bring a medium saucepan of water to the boil. Add the wontons and return to the boil. Simmer for 2–3 minutes, or until the wontons are cooked, stirring frequently. Rinse under cold running water, drain and reserve.

4 Pour 300 ml/$^1/_2$ pint stock per person into a large wok. Bring to the boil over a high heat, skimming any foam that rises to the surface and simmer for 5–7 minutes to reduce slightly. Add the wontons, Chinese leaves or spinach, carrots and spring onions. Season with a few drops of soy sauce and simmer for 2–3 minutes. Garnish with a few parsley leaves and serve immediately.

Ingredients   SERVES 6

For the chicken stock:
900 g/2 lb chicken or chicken pieces
    with back, feet and wings
1–2 onions, peeled and quartered
2 carrots, peeled and chopped
2 celery stalks, trimmed and chopped
1 leek, trimmed and chopped
2 garlic cloves, unpeeled, lightly crushed
1 tbsp black peppercorns
2 bay leaves
small bunch parsley, stems only
2–3 slices fresh root ginger,
    peeled (optional)
3.4 litres/6 pints cold water

For the soup:
18 wontons
2–3 Chinese leaves, or a handful
    of spinach, shredded
1 small carrot, peeled and cut
    into matchsticks
2–4 spring onions, trimmed and
    diagonally sliced
soy sauce, to taste
handful of flat–leaf parsley, to garnish

Thai Hot-&-Sour Prawn Soup

1 Remove the heads from the prawns by twisting away from the body and reserve. Peel the prawns, leaving the tails on and reserve the shells with the heads. Using a sharp knife, remove the black vein from the back of the prawns. Rinse and dry the prawns and reserve. Rinse and dry the heads and shells.

2 Heat a wok, add the oil and, when hot, add the prawn heads and shells, the lemon grass, ginger, garlic, coriander stems and black pepper and stir–fry for 2–3 minutes, or until the prawn heads and shells turn pink and all the ingredients are coloured.

3 Carefully add the water to the wok and return to the boil, skimming off any scum which rises to the surface. Simmer over a medium heat for 10 minutes or until slightly reduced. Strain through a fine sieve and return the clear prawn stock to the wok.

4 Bring the stock back to the boil and add the reserved prawns, chillies, lime leaves and spring onions and simmer for 3 minutes, or until the prawns turn pink. Season with the fish sauce and lime juice. Spoon into heated soup bowls, dividing the prawns evenly and float a few coriander leaves over the surface.

Ingredients   SERVES 6

700 g/1^1/$_2$ lb large raw prawns

2 tbsp vegetable oil

3–4 stalks lemon grass, outer leaves discarded, and coarsely chopped

2.5 cm/1 inch piece fresh root ginger, peeled and finely chopped

2–3 garlic cloves, peeled and crushed

small bunch fresh coriander, leaves stripped and reserved, stems finely chopped

^{1}/$_2$ tsp freshly ground black pepper

1.8 litres/3^1/$_4$ pints water

1–2 small red chillies, deseeded and thinly sliced

1–2 small green chillies, deseeded and thinly sliced

6 kaffir lime leaves, thinly shredded

4 spring onions, trimmed and diagonally sliced

1–2 tbsp Thai fish sauce

1–2 tbsp freshly squeezed lime juice

Food fact

Thai fish sauce, made from fermented anchovies, has a sour, salty, fishy flavour.

Creamy Caribbean Chicken & Coconut Soup

1 Trim the spring onions and slice thinly; peel the garlic and chop finely. Cut off the top of the chilli, slit down the side and remove seeds and membrane, then chop finely and reserve.

2 Remove and discard any skin or bones from the cooked chicken, shred using two forks and reserve.

3 Heat a large wok, add the oil and, when hot, add the spring onions, garlic and chilli and stir–fry for 2 minutes, or until the onion has softened. Stir in the turmeric and cook for 1 minute.

4 Blend the coconut milk with the chicken stock until smooth, then pour into the wok. Add the pasta or spaghetti with the lemon slices and bring to the boil.

5 Simmer, half–covered, for 10–12 minutes, or until the pasta is tender; stir occasionally.

6 Remove the lemon slices from the wok and add the chicken. Season to taste with salt and pepper and simmer for 2–3 minutes, or until the chicken is heated through thoroughly.

7 Stir in the chopped coriander and ladle into heated bowls. Garnish with sprigs of fresh coriander and serve immediately.

Ingredients SERVES 4

6–8 spring onions
2 garlic cloves
1 red chilli
175 g/6 oz cooked chicken, shredded or diced
2 tbsp vegetable oil
1 tsp ground turmeric
300 ml/^{1}/$_2$ pint coconut milk
900 ml/1^1/$_2$ pints chicken stock
50 g/2 oz small soup pasta or spaghetti, broken into small pieces
^{1}/$_2$ lemon, sliced
salt and freshly ground black pepper
1–2 tbsp freshly chopped coriander
sprigs of fresh coriander, to garnish

Helpful hint

Be careful handling chillies. Either wear rubber gloves or scrub your hands thoroughly, using plenty of soap and water. Avoid touching eyes or any other sensitive areas.

Sweetcorn & Crab Soup

1 Wash and dry the corns cobs. Using a sharp knife and holding the corn cobs at an angle to the cutting board, cut down along the cobs to remove the kernels, then scrape the cobs to remove any excess milky residue. Put the kernels and the milky residue into a large wok.

2 Add the chicken stock to the wok and place over a high heat. Bring to the boil, stirring and pressing some of the kernels against the side of the wok to squeeze out the starch to help thicken the soup. Simmer for 15 minutes, stirring occasionally.

3 Add the spring onions, ginger, sherry or Chinese rice wine, soy sauce and brown sugar to the wok and season to taste with salt and pepper. Simmer for a further 5 minutes, stirring occasionally.

4 Blend the cornflour with 1 tablespoon of cold water to form a smooth paste and whisk into the soup. Return to the boil, then simmer over a medium heat until thickened.

5 Add the crab meat, stirring until blended. Beat the egg white with the sesame oil and stir into the soup in a slow, steady stream, stirring constantly. Stir in the chopped coriander and serve immediately.

Ingredients   SERVES 4

450 g/1 lb fresh corn on the cob

1.3 litres/2$^{1}/_{4}$ pints chicken stock

2–3 spring onions, trimmed and
  finely chopped

1 cm/$^{1}/_{2}$ inch piece fresh root ginger,
  peeled and finely chopped

1 tbsp dry sherry or Chinese
  rice wine

2–3 tsp soy sauce

1 tsp soft light brown sugar

salt and freshly ground black pepper

2 tsp cornflour

225 g/8 oz white crab meat,
  fresh or canned

1 medium egg white

1 tsp sesame oil

1–2 tbsp freshly chopped coriander

Tasty tip

For chicken stock that is home–made, follow the instructions for Wonton Soup (see page 56).

Hot-&-Sour Soup

1 Place the dried Chinese (shiitake) mushrooms in a small bowl and pour over enough almost–boiling water to cover. Leave for 20 minutes to soften, then gently lift out and squeeze out the liquid. (Lifting out the mushrooms leaves any grit behind.) Discard the stems and thinly slice the caps and reserve.

2 Heat a large wok, add the oil and, when hot, add the carrot strips and stir–fry for 2–3 minutes, or until beginning to soften. Add the chestnut mushrooms and stir–fry for 2–3 minutes or until golden, then stir in the garlic and chillies.

3 Add the chicken stock to the vegetables and bring to the boil, skimming off any foam that rises to the surface. Add the shredded chicken or pork, bean curd, if using, spring onions, sugar, vinegar, soy sauce and reserved Chinese mushrooms and simmer for 5 minutes, stirring occasionally. Season to taste with salt and pepper.

4 Blend the cornflour with 1 tablespoon of cold water to form a smooth paste and whisk into the soup. Return to the boil and simmer over a medium heat until thickened.

5 Beat the egg with the sesame oil and slowly add to the soup in a slow, steady stream, stirring constantly. Stir in the chopped coriander and serve the soup immediately.

Ingredients   SERVES 4–6

25 g/1 oz dried Chinese (shiitake) mushrooms
2 tbsp groundnut oil
1 carrot, peeled and cut into julienne strips
125 g/4 oz chestnut mushrooms, wiped and thinly sliced
2 garlic cloves, peeled and finely chopped
$^{1}/_{2}$ tsp dried crushed chillies
1.1 litres/2 pints chicken stock (see page 56)
75 g/3 oz cooked boneless chicken or pork, shredded
125 g/4 oz fresh bean curd, thinly sliced (optional)
2–3 spring onions, trimmed and finely sliced diagonally
1–2 tsp sugar
3 tbsp cider vinegar
2 tbsp soy sauce
salt and freshly ground black pepper
1 tbsp cornflour
1 large egg
2 tsp sesame oil
2 tbsp freshly chopped coriander

Chinese Leaf & Mushroom Soup

1 Trim the stem ends of the Chinese leaves and cut in half lengthways. Remove the triangular core with a knife, then cut into 2.5 cm/1 inch slices and reserve.

2 Place the dried Chinese mushrooms in a bowl and pour over enough almost–boiling water to cover. Leave to stand for 20 minutes to soften, then gently lift out and squeeze out the liquid. Discard the stems and thinly slice the caps and reserve. Strain the liquid through a muslin–lined sieve or a coffee filter paper and reserve.

3 Heat a wok over a medium–high heat, add the oil and, when hot, add the bacon. Stir–fry for 3–4 minutes, or until crisp and golden, stirring frequently. Add the ginger and chestnut mushrooms and stir–fry for a further 2–3 minutes.

4 Add the chicken stock and bring to the boil, skimming off any fat and scum that rises to the surface. Add the spring onions, sherry or rice wine, Chinese leaves and sliced Chinese mushrooms and season to taste with salt and pepper. Pour in the reserved soaking liquid and reduce the heat to the lowest possible setting.

5 Simmer gently, covered, until all the vegetables are very tender; this will take about 10 minutes. Add a little water if the liquid has reduced too much. Spoon into soup bowls and drizzle with a little sesame oil. Serve immediately.

Ingredients   SERVES 4–6

450 g/1 lb Chinese leaves
25 g/1 oz dried Chinese (shiitake) mushrooms
1 tbsp vegetable oil
75 g/3 oz smoked streaky bacon, diced
2.5 cm/1 inch piece fresh root ginger, peeled and finely chopped
175 g/6 oz chestnut mushrooms, thinly sliced
1.1 litres/2 pints chicken stock
4–6 spring onions, trimmed and cut into short lengths
2 tbsp dry sherry or Chinese rice wine
salt and freshly ground black pepper
sesame oil, for drizzling

Tasty tip
If Chinese leaves are not available, use Savoy cabbage.

1

3

4

Vietnamese Beef & Rice Noodle Soup

1   Place all the ingredients for the beef stock into a large stock pot or saucepan and cover with cold water. Bring to the boil and skim off any scum that rises to the surface. Reduce the heat and simmer gently, partially covered, for 2–3 hours, skimming occasionally.

2   Strain into a large bowl and leave to cool, then skim off the fat. Chill in the refrigerator and, when cold, remove any fat from the surface. Pour 1.7 litres/3 pints of the stock into a large wok and reserve.

3   Cover the noodles with warm water and leave for 3 minutes, or until just softened. Drain, then cut into 10 cm/4 inch lengths.

4   Arrange the spring onions and chilli on a serving platter or large plate. Strip the leaves from the coriander and mint and arrange them in piles on the plate.

5   Bring the stock in the wok to the boil over a high heat. Add the noodles and simmer for about 2 minutes, or until tender. Add the beef strips and simmer for about 1 minute. Season to taste with salt and pepper.

6   Ladle the soup with the noodles and beef strips into individual soup bowls and serve immediately with the plate of condiments handed around separately.

Ingredients   SERVES 4–6

For the beef stock:
900 g/2 lb meaty beef bones
1 large onion, peeled and quartered
2 carrots, peeled and cut into chunks
2 celery stalks, trimmed and sliced
1 leek, washed and sliced into chunks
2 garlic cloves, unpeeled and
    lightly crushed
3 whole star anise
1 tsp black peppercorns

For the soup:
175 g/6 oz dried rice stick noodles
4–6 spring onions, trimmed and
    diagonally sliced
1 red chilli, deseeded and
    diagonally sliced
1 small bunch fresh coriander
1 small bunch fresh mint
350 g/12 oz fillet steak, very
    thinly sliced
salt and freshly ground black pepper

3

4

5

Laksa Malayan Rice Noodle Soup

1   Put the chicken in a large saucepan with the peppercorns and cover with cold water. Bring to the boil, skimming off any scum that rises to the surface. Simmer, partially covered, for about 1 hour. Remove the chicken and cool. Skim any fat from the stock and strain through a muslin-lined sieve and reserve. Remove the meat from the carcass, shred and reserve.

2   Heat a large wok, add the oil and, when hot, add the onions and stir-fry for 2 minutes, or until they begin to colour. Stir in the garlic, ginger, coriander, chillies and curry paste and stir-fry for a further 2 minutes.

3   Carefully pour in the reserved stock (you need at least 1.1 litres/2 pints) and simmer gently, partially covered, for 10 minutes, or until slightly reduced.

4   Add the coconut milk, prawns, Chinese leaves, sugar, spring onions and bean sprouts and simmer for 3 minutes, stirring occasionally. Add the reserved shredded chicken and cook for a further 2 minutes.

5   Drain the noodles and divide between four to six soup bowls. Ladle the hot stock and vegetables over the noodles, making sure each serving has some prawns and chicken. Garnish each bowl with fresh mint leaves and serve immediately.

Ingredients   SERVES 4–6

1.1 kg/2$^1/_2$ lb corn-fed, free-range chicken
1 tsp black peppercorns
1 tbsp vegetable oil
1 large onion, peeled and thinly sliced
2 garlic cloves, peeled and finely chopped
2.5 cm/1 inch piece fresh root ginger, peeled and thinly sliced
1 tsp ground coriander
2 red chillies, deseeded and diagonally sliced
1–2 tsp hot curry paste
400 ml/14 fl oz coconut milk
450 g/1 lb large raw prawns, peeled and deveined
$^1/_2$ small head of Chinese leaves, thinly shredded
1 tsp sugar
2 spring onions, trimmed and thinly sliced
125 g/4 oz bean sprouts
250 g/9 oz rice noodles or rice sticks, soaked as per packet instructions
fresh mint leaves, to garnish

Sour-&-Spicy Prawn Soup

1 Place the noodles in cold water and leave to soak while preparing the soup. Place the dried mushrooms in a small bowl, cover with almost–boiling water and leave for 20–30 minutes. Drain, strain and reserve the soaking liquid and discard any woody stems from the mushrooms.

2 Finely shred the spring onions and place into a small bowl. Cover with ice–cold water and refrigerate until required and the spring onions have curled.

3 Place the green chillies with 2 tablespoons of the chopped coriander in a pestle and mortar and pound to a paste. Reserve.

4 Pour the stock into a saucepan and bring gently to the boil. Stir in the ginger, lemon grass and lime leaves with the reserved mushrooms and their liquid. Return to the boil.

5 Drain the noodles, add to the soup with the prawns, Thai fish sauce and lime juice and then stir in the chilli and coriander paste. Bring to the boil, then simmer for 3 minutes. Stir in the remaining chopped coriander and season to taste with salt and pepper. Ladle into warmed bowls, sprinkle with the spring onion curls and serve immediately.

Ingredients   SERVES 4

50 g/2 oz rice noodles
25 g/1 oz Chinese dried mushrooms
4 spring onions, trimmed
2 small green chillies
3 tbsp freshly chopped coriander
600 ml/1 pint chicken stock
2.5 cm/1 inch piece fresh root ginger, peeled and grated
2 lemon grass stalks, outer leaves discarded, and finely chopped
4 kaffir lime leaves
12 raw king prawns, peeled with tail shell left on
2 tbsp Thai fish sauce
2 tbsp lime juice
salt and freshly ground black pepper

Helpful hint

After soaking the mushrooms, rinse them under cold running water to remove any traces of grit. Also strain the soaking liquid through a very fine sieve or a piece of muslin before adding to the stock.

White Bean Soup with Parmesan Croutons

1 Preheat the oven to 200°C/400°F/Gas Mark 6. Place the cubes of bread in a bowl and pour over the groundnut oil. Stir to coat the bread, then sprinkle over the Parmesan cheese. Place on a lightly oiled baking tray and bake in the preheated oven for 10 minutes, or until crisp and golden.

2 Heat the olive oil in a large saucepan and cook the onion for 4–5 minutes until softened. Add the bacon and thyme and cook for a further 3 minutes. Stir in the beans, stock and black pepper and simmer gently for 5 minutes.

3 Place half the bean mixture and liquid into a food processor and blend until smooth.

4 Return the purée to the saucepan. Stir in the pesto sauce, pepperoni sausage and lemon juice and season to taste with salt and pepper.

5 Return the soup to the heat and cook for a further 2–3 minutes, or until piping hot. Place some of the beans in each serving bowl and add a ladleful of soup. Garnish with shredded basil and serve immediately with the croutons scattered over the top.

Ingredients SERVES 4

3 thick slices of white bread, cut into
  1 cm/½ inch cubes
3 tbsp groundnut oil
2 tbsp Parmesan cheese, finely
  grated
1 tbsp light olive oil
1 large onion, peeled and finely
  chopped
50 g/2 oz unsmoked bacon lardons
  (or thick slices of bacon, diced)
1 tbsp fresh thyme leaves
2 x 400 g tins cannellini beans,
  drained
900 ml/1½ pints chicken stock
salt and freshly ground black pepper
1 tbsp prepared pesto sauce
50 g/2 oz piece of pepperoni
  sausage, diced
1 tbsp fresh lemon juice
1 tbsp fresh basil, roughly shredded

Rice Soup with Potato Sticks

1 Preheat the oven to 190°C/375°F/Gas Mark 5. Heat 25 g/1 oz of the butter and the olive oil in a saucepan and cook the onion for 4–5 minutes until softened, then add the Parma ham and cook for about 1 minute. Stir in the rice, the stock and the peas. Season to taste with salt and pepper and simmer for 10–15 minutes, or until the rice is tender.

2 Beat the egg and 125 g/4 oz of the butter together until smooth, then beat in the flour, a pinch of salt and the potato. Work the ingredients together to form a soft, pliable dough, adding a little more flour if necessary.

3 Roll the dough out on a lightly floured surface into a rectangle 1 cm/½ inch thick and cut into 12 thin long sticks. Brush with milk and sprinkle on the poppy seeds. Place the sticks on a lightly oiled baking tray and bake in the preheated oven for 15 minutes, or until golden.

4 When the rice is cooked, stir the remaining butter and Parmesan cheese into the soup and sprinkle the chopped parsley over the top. Serve immediately with the warm potato sticks.

Ingredients   SERVES 4

175 g/6 oz butter
1 tsp olive oil
1 large onion, peeled and
    finely chopped
4 slices Parma ham, chopped
100 g/3½ oz Arborio rice
1.1 litres/2 pints chicken stock
350 g/12 oz frozen peas
salt and freshly ground black pepper
1 medium egg
125 g/4 oz self-raising flour
175 g/6 oz mashed potato
1 tbsp milk
1 tbsp poppy seeds
1 tbsp Parmesan cheese,
    finely grated
1 tbsp freshly chopped parsley

Tasty tip

These potato sticks also make a delicious snack with drinks. Try sprinkling them with sesame seeds or grated cheese and allow to cool before serving.

Rich Tomato Soup with Roasted Red Peppers

1 Preheat the oven to 200°C/400°F/Gas Mark 6. Lightly oil a roasting tin with 1 teaspoon of the olive oil. Place the peppers and tomatoes cut-side down in the roasting tin with the onion quarters and the garlic cloves. Spoon over the remaining oil.

2 Bake in the preheated oven for 30 minutes, or until the skins on the peppers have started to blacken and blister. Allow the vegetables to cool for about 10 minutes, then remove the skins, stalks and seeds from the peppers. Peel away the skins from the tomatoes and onions and squeeze out the garlic.

3 Place the cooked vegetables into a blender or food processor and blend until smooth. Add the stock and blend again to form a smooth purée. Pour the puréed soup through a sieve, if a smooth soup is preferred, then pour into a saucepan. Bring to the boil, simmer gently for 2–3 minutes, and season to taste with salt and pepper. Serve hot with a swirl of soured cream and a sprinkling of shredded basil on the top.

Ingredients   SERVES 4

2 tsp light olive oil
700 g/1½ lb red peppers, halved and deseeded
450 g/1 lb ripe plum tomatoes, halved
2 onions, unpeeled and quartered
4 garlic cloves, unpeeled
600 ml/1 pint chicken stock
salt and freshly ground black pepper
4 tbsp soured cream
1 tbsp freshly shredded basil

Helpful hint

A quick, hassle-free way to remove the skin from peppers once they have been roasted or grilled is to place them in a polythene bag. Leave for 10 minutes or until cool enough to handle, then simply peel the skin away from the flesh.

Rocket & Potato Soup with Garlic Croutons

1 Place the potatoes in a large saucepan, cover with the stock and simmer gently for 10 minutes. Add the rocket leaves and simmer for a further 5–10 minutes, or until the potatoes are soft and the rocket has wilted.

2 Meanwhile, make the croutons. Cut the thick, white sliced bread into small cubes and reserve. Heat the butter and groundnut oil in a small frying pan and cook the garlic for 1 minute, stirring well. Remove the garlic. Add the bread cubes to the butter and oil mixture in the frying pan and sauté, stirring continuously, until they are golden brown. Drain the croutons on absorbent kitchen paper and reserve.

3 Cut the ciabatta bread into small dice and stir into the soup. Cover the saucepan and leave to stand for 10 minutes, or until the bread has absorbed a lot of the liquid.

4 Stir in the olive oil, season to taste with salt and pepper and serve at once with a few of the garlic croutons scattered over the top and a little grated Parmesan cheese.

Ingredients   SERVES 4

700 g/1¹/₂ lb baby new potatoes
1.1 litres/2 pints chicken or
   vegetable stock
50 g/2 oz rocket leaves
125 g/4 oz thick white sliced bread
50 g/2 oz unsalted butter
1 tsp groundnut oil
2–4 garlic cloves, peeled
   and chopped
125 g/4 oz stale ciabatta bread,
   with the crusts removed
4 tbsp olive oil
salt and freshly ground black pepper
2 tbsp Parmesan cheese,
   finely grated

Helpful hint

Rocket is now widely available in bags from most large supermarkets. If, however, you cannot get hold of it, replace it with an equal quantity of watercress or baby spinach leaves.

Classic Minestrone

1. Heat the butter and olive oil together in a large saucepan. Chop the bacon and add to the saucepan. Cook for 3–4 minutes, then remove with a slotted spoon and reserve.

2. Finely chop the onion, garlic, celery and carrots and add to the saucepan, one ingredient at a time, stirring well after each addition. Cover and cook gently for 8–10 minutes, until the vegetables are softened.

3. Add the chopped tomatoes, with their juice and the stock, bring to the boil, then cover the saucepan with a lid, reduce the heat and simmer gently for about 20 minutes.

4. Stir in the cabbage, beans, peas and spaghetti pieces. Cover and simmer for a further 20 minutes, or until all the ingredients are tender. Season to taste with salt and pepper.

5. Return the cooked bacon to the saucepan and bring the soup to the boil. Serve the soup immediately with Parmesan cheese shavings sprinkled on the top and plenty of crusty bread to accompany it.

Ingredients   SERVES 6–8

25 g/1 oz butter
3 tbsp olive oil
3 rashers streaky bacon
1 large onion, peeled
1 garlic clove, peeled
1 celery stick, trimmed
2 carrots, peeled
400 g can chopped tomatoes
1.1 litres/2 pints chicken stock
175 g/6 oz green cabbage,
    finely shredded
50 g/2 oz French beans, trimmed
    and halved
3 tbsp frozen petits pois
50 g/2 oz spaghetti, broken into
    short pieces
salt and freshly ground black pepper
Parmesan cheese shavings, to garnish
crusty bread, to serve

Cream of Pumpkin Soup

1 Cut the skinned and deseeded pumpkin flesh into 2.5 cm/1 inch cubes. Heat the olive oil in a large saucepan and cook the pumpkin for 2–3 minutes, coating it completely with oil. Chop the onion and leek finely and cut the carrot and celery into small dice.

2 Add the vegetables to the saucepan with the garlic and cook, stirring, for 5 minutes, or until they have begun to soften. Cover the vegetables with the water and bring to the boil. Season with plenty of salt and pepper and the nutmeg, cover and simmer for 15–20 minutes, or until all of the vegetables are tender.

3 When the vegetables are tender, remove from the heat, cool slightly then pour into a food processor or blender. Liquidise to form a smooth purée then pass through a sieve back into the saucepan.

4 Adjust the seasoning to taste and add all but 2 tablespoons of the cream and enough water to obtain the correct consistency. Bring the soup to boiling point, add the cayenne pepper and serve immediately swirled with cream and warm herby bread.

Ingredients   SERVES 4

900 g/2 lb pumpkin flesh (after peeling and discarding the seeds)
4 tbsp olive oil
1 large onion, peeled
1 leek, trimmed
1 carrot, peeled
2 celery sticks
4 garlic cloves, peeled and crushed
1.7 litres/3 pints water
salt and freshly ground black pepper
$^1/_4$ tsp freshly grated nutmeg
150 ml/$^1/_4$ pint single cream
$^1/_4$ tsp cayenne pepper
warm herby bread, to serve

Tasty tip

If you cannot find pumpkin, try replacing it with squash. Butternut, acorn or turban squash would all make suitable substitutes. Avoid spaghetti squash which is not firm–fleshed when cooked.

Starters

This section contains a wide selection of tasty dishes that can be prepared as starters or are ideal as snacks whenever a full meal is not required. Influences from around the world come together to tantalize the taste buds, from Thai Fish Cakes and Roasted Aubergine Dip with Pitta Strips, to Spicy Beef Pancakes and Sticky Braised Spare Ribs.

Mushroom & Red Wine Pâté

1 Preheat the oven to 180°C/350°F/Gas Mark 4. Cut the bread in half diagonally. Place the bread triangles on a baking tray and cook for 10 minutes.

2 Remove from the oven and split each bread triangle in half to make 12 triangles and return to the oven until golden and crisp. Leave to cool on a wire rack.

3 Heat the oil in a saucepan and gently cook the onion and garlic until transparent.

4 Add the mushrooms and cook, stirring, for 3–4 minutes or until the mushroom juices start to run.

5 Stir the wine and herbs into the mushroom mixture and bring to the boil. Reduce the heat and simmer uncovered until all the liquid is absorbed.

6 Remove from the heat and season to taste with salt and pepper. Leave to cool.

7 When cold, beat in the soft cream cheese and adjust the seasoning. Place in a small clean bowl and chill until required. Serve the toast triangles with the cucumber and tomato.

Ingredients SERVES 4

3 large slices of white bread,
   crusts removed
2 tsp oil
1 small onion, peeled and
   finely chopped
1 garlic clove, peeled and crushed
350 g/12 oz button mushrooms,
   wiped and finely chopped
150 ml/$^1/_4$ pint red wine
$^1/_2$ tsp dried mixed herbs
1 tbsp freshly chopped parsley
salt and freshly ground black pepper
2 tbsp cream cheese

To serve:
finely chopped cucumber
finely chopped tomato

Food fact
This pâté is also delicious served as a bruschetta topping. Toast slices of ciabatta, generously spread the pâté on top and garnish with a little rocket.

Thai Fish Cakes

1   Preheat the oven to 190°C/375°F/Gas Mark 5. Place the chilli, coriander, garlic, spring onions and lemon grass in a food processor and blend together.

2   Pat the prawns and cod dry with kitchen paper.

3   Add to the food processor and blend until the mixture is roughly chopped.

4   Season to taste with salt and pepper and blend to mix.

5   Dampen your hands, then shape heaped tablespoons of the mixture into 12 little patties.

6   Place the patties on a lightly oiled baking sheet and cook in the preheated oven for 12–15 minutes or until piping hot and cooked through. Turn the patties over halfway through the cooking time.

7   Serve the fish cakes immediately with the sweet chilli sauce for dipping.

Ingredients   SERVES 4

1 red chilli, deseeded and roughly chopped
4 tbsp roughly chopped fresh coriander
1 garlic clove, peeled and crushed
2 spring onions, trimmed and roughly chopped
1 lemon grass stalk, outer leaves discarded, and roughly chopped
75 g/3 oz prawns, thawed if frozen
275 g/10 oz cod fillet, skinned, pin bones removed and cubed
salt and freshly ground black pepper
sweet chilli dipping sauce, to serve

Tasty tip

A horseradish accompaniment could be used in place of the sweet chilli sauce if a creamier dip is preferred. Mix together 2 tablespoons of grated horseradish (from a jar) with 3 tablespoons each of Greek yogurt and mayonnaise. Add 3 finely chopped spring onions, a squeeze of lime and salt and pepper to taste.

1

2

5

Hoisin Chicken Pancakes

1 Preheat the oven to 190°C/375°F/Gas Mark 5. In a non-metallic bowl, mix the hoisin sauce with the garlic, ginger, soy sauce, sesame oil and seasoning.

2 Add the chicken thighs and turn to coat in the mixture. Cover loosely and leave in the refrigerator to marinate for 3–4 hours, turning the chicken from time to time.

3 Remove the chicken from the marinade and place in a roasting tin. Reserve the marinade. Bake in the preheated oven for 30 minutes basting occasionally with the marinade.

4 Cut the cucumber in half lengthways and remove the seeds by running a teaspoon down the middle to scoop them out. Cut into thin batons.

5 Place the pancakes in a steamer to warm or heat according to packet instructions. Thinly slice the hot chicken and arrange on a plate with the shredded spring onions, cucumber and pancakes.

6 Place a spoonful of the chicken in the middle of each warmed pancake and top with pieces of cucumber, spring onion and a little dipping sauce. Roll up and serve immediately.

Ingredients   SERVES 4

3 tbsp hoisin sauce
1 garlic clove, peeled and crushed
2.5 cm/1 inch piece root ginger, peeled and finely grated
1 tbsp soy sauce
1 tsp sesame oil
salt and freshly ground black pepper
4 skinless chicken thighs
$^1/_2$ cucumber, peeled (optional)
12 bought Chinese pancakes
6 spring onions, trimmed and cut lengthways into fine shreds
sweet chilli dipping sauce, to serve

Tasty tip

For those with wheat allergies or who want to make this tasty dish more substantial, stir-fry the spring onions and cucumber batons in a little groundnut oil. Add a carrot cut into batons and mix in the thinly sliced chicken and reserved marinade (as prepared in step 3). Serve with steamed rice – Thai fragrant rice is particularly good.

Hot Herby Mushrooms

1 Preheat the oven to 180°C/350°F/Gas Mark 4. With a rolling pin, roll each piece of bread out as thinly as possible.

2 Press each piece of bread into a 10 cm/4 inch tartlet tin. Push each piece down firmly, then bake in the preheated oven for 20 minutes.

3 Place the mushrooms in a frying pan with the garlic, mustard and chicken stock and stir-fry over a moderate heat until the mushrooms are tender and the liquid is reduced by half.

4 Carefully remove the mushrooms from the frying pan with a slotted spoon and transfer to a heat-resistant dish. Cover with foil and place in the bottom of the oven to keep the mushrooms warm.

5 Boil the remaining pan juices until reduced to a thick sauce. Season with salt and pepper.

6 Stir the parsley and the chives into the mushroom mixture.

7 Place one bread tartlet case on each plate and divide the mushroom mixture between them.

8 Spoon over the pan juices, garnish with the chives and serve immediately with mixed salad leaves.

Ingredients   SERVES 4

4 thin slices of white bread, crusts removed
125 g/4 oz chestnut mushrooms, wiped and sliced
125 g/4 oz oyster mushrooms, wiped
1 garlic clove, peeled and crushed
1 tsp Dijon mustard
300 ml/^{1}/$_2$ pint chicken stock
salt and freshly ground black pepper
1 tbsp freshly chopped parsley
1 tbsp freshly snipped chives, plus extra to garnish
mixed salad leaves, to serve

Food fact

Mushrooms are an extremely nutritious food, rich in vitamins and minerals, which help to boost our immune system. This recipe could be adapted to include shiitake mushrooms which studies have shown can significantly boost and protect the body's immune system and can go some way to boost the body's protection against cancer.

Coriander Chicken & Soy Sauce Cakes

1   Preheat the oven to 190°C/375°F/Gas Mark 5. Halve the cucumber lengthwise, deseed and dice.

2   In a bowl, mix the shallot and radishes. Chill until ready to serve with the diced cucumber.

3   Place the chicken thighs in a food processor and blend until coarsely chopped.

4   Add the coriander and spring onions to the chicken with the chilli, lime rind and soy sauce. Blend again until mixed.

5   Using slightly damp hands, shape the chicken mixture into 12 small rounds.

6   Place the rounds on a lightly oiled baking tray and bake in the preheated for 15 minutes, until golden.

7   In a small pan, heat the sugar with 2 tablespoons of water until dissolved. Simmer until syrupy.

8   Remove from the heat and allow to cool a little, then stir in the vinegar and chilli slices. Pour over the cucumber and the radish and shallot salad. Garnish with the chopped coriander and serve the chicken cakes with the salad immediately.

Ingredients   SERVES 4

$1/4$ cucumber, peeled
1 shallot, peeled and thinly sliced
6 radishes, trimmed and sliced
350 g/12 oz skinless boneless
   chicken thigh
4 tbsp fresh coriander,
   roughly chopped
2 spring onions, trimmed and
   roughly chopped
1 red chilli, deseeded and chopped
finely grated rind of $1/2$ lime
2 tbsp soy sauce
1 tbsp caster sugar
2 tbsp rice vinegar
1 red chilli, deseeded and
   finely sliced
freshly chopped coriander, to garnish

Food fact

In this recipe, the chicken cakes can be altered so that half chicken and half lean pork is used. This alters the flavour of the dish and works really well if a small 2.5 cm/1 inch piece of fresh ginger is grated and added in step 4.

Roasted Aubergine Dip with Pitta Strips

1   Preheat the oven to 180°C/350°F/Gas Mark 4. On a chopping board, cut the pitta breads into strips. Spread the bread in a single layer on to a large baking tray.

2   Cook in the preheated oven for 15 minutes until golden and crisp. Leave to cool on a wire cooling rack.

3   Trim the aubergines, rinse lightly and reserve. Heat a griddle pan until almost smoking. Cook the aubergines and garlic for about 15 minutes.

4   Turn the aubergines frequently, until very tender with wrinkled and charred skins. Remove from the heat. Leave to cool.

5   When the aubergines are cool enough to handle, cut in half and scoop out the cooked flesh and place in a food processor.

6   Squeeze the softened garlic flesh from the papery skin and add to the aubergine.

7   Blend the aubergine and garlic until smooth, then add the sesame oil, lemon juice and cumin and blend again to mix.

8   Season to taste with salt and pepper, stir in the parsley and serve with the pitta strips and mixed salad leaves.

Ingredients   SERVES 4

4 pitta breads
2 large aubergines
1 garlic clove, peeled
$\frac{1}{4}$ tsp sesame oil
1 tbsp lemon juice
$\frac{1}{2}$ tsp ground cumin
salt and freshly ground black pepper
2 tbsp freshly chopped parsley
fresh salad leaves, to serve

Griddled Garlic & Lemon Squid

1 Rinse the rice until the water runs clear, then place in a saucepan with the stock.

2 Bring to the boil, then reduce the heat. Cover and simmer gently for 10 minutes.

3 Turn off the heat and leave the pan covered so the rice can steam while you cook the squid.

4 Remove the tentacles from the squid and reserve.

5 Cut the body cavity in half. Using the tip of a small sharp knife, score the inside flesh of the body cavity in a diamond pattern. Do not cut all the way through.

6 Mix the lemon rind, crushed garlic and chopped shallot together.

7 Place the squid in a shallow bowl, sprinkle over the lemon mixture and stir.

8 Heat a griddle pan until almost smoking. Cook the squid for 3–4 minutes until cooked through, then slice.

9 Sprinkle with the coriander and lemon juice. Season to taste with salt and pepper. Drain the rice and serve immediately with the squid.

Ingredients   SERVES 4

125 g/4 oz long–grain rice
300 ml/$^1/_2$ pint fish stock
225 g/8 oz squid, cleaned
finely grated rind of 1 lemon
1 garlic clove, peeled and crushed
1 shallot, peeled and finely chopped
2 tbsp freshly chopped coriander
2 tbsp lemon juice
salt and freshly ground black pepper

Helpful hint

To prepare squid, peel the tentacles from the squid's pouch and cut away the head just below the eye. Discard the head. Remove the quill and the soft innards from the squid and discard. Peel off any dark skin that covers the squid and discard. Rinse the tentacles and pouch thoroughly. The squid is now ready to use.

Creamy Salmon with Dill in Filo Baskets

1 Preheat the oven to 200°C/400°F/Gas Mark 6. Place the bay leaf, peppercorns, parsley and salmon in a frying pan and add enough water to barely cover the fish.

2 Bring to the boil, reduce the heat and poach the fish for 5 minutes until it flakes easily. Remove it from the pan. Reserve.

3 Brush each sheet of filo pastry lightly with the oil. Scrunch up the pastry to make a nest shape approximately 12.5 cm/5 inches in diameter.

4 Place on a lightly oiled baking sheet and cook in the preheated oven for 10 minutes until golden and crisp.

5 Blanch the spinach in a pan of lightly salted boiling water for 2 minutes. Drain thoroughly and keep warm.

6 Mix the fromage frais, mustard and dill together, then warm gently. Season to taste with salt and pepper. Divide the spinach between the filo pastry nests and flake the salmon on to the spinach.

7 Spoon the mustard and dill sauce over the filo baskets and serve immediately.

Ingredients
SERVES 4

1 bay leaf
6 black peppercorns
1 large sprig fresh parsley
175 g/6 oz salmon fillet
4 large sheets filo pastry
2 tsp sunflower oil
125 g/4 oz baby spinach leaves
8 tbsp fromage frais
2 tsp Dijon mustard
2 tbsp freshly chopped dill
salt and freshly ground black pepper

Food fact
This is a highly nutritious dish combining calcium–rich salmon with vitamin and mineral–rich spinach. The fromage frais in this recipe can be substituted for live yogurt if you want to aid digestion and give the immune system a real boost.

Smoked Salmon Sushi

1   Rinse the rice thoroughly in cold water, until the water runs clear, then place in a pan with 300 ml/$\frac{1}{2}$ pint of water. Bring to the boil and cover with a tight-fitting lid. Reduce to a simmer and cook gently for 10 minutes. Turn the heat off, but keep the pan covered, to allow the rice to steam for a further 10 minutes.

2   In a small saucepan, gently heat the rice vinegar, sugar and salt until the sugar has dissolved. When the rice has finished steaming, pour over the vinegar mixture and stir well to mix. Empty the rice out on to a large flat surface – a chopping board or large plate is ideal. Fan the rice to cool and to make it shiny.

3   Lay one sheet of sushi nori on a sushi mat (if you do not have a sushi mat, improvise with a stiff piece of fabric that is a little larger than the sushi nori) and spread with half the cooled rice. Dampen the hands while doing this – it will help to prevent the rice from sticking to your hands. On the nearest edge, place half the salmon and half the cucumber strips.

4   Roll up the rice and smoked salmon into a tight Swiss roll–like shape. Dampen the blade of a sharp knife and cut the sushi into slices about 2 cm/$\frac{3}{4}$ inch thick. Repeat with the remaining sushi nori, rice, smoked salmon and cucumber. Serve with wasabi, soy sauce and pickled ginger.

Ingredients   SERVES 4

175 g/6 oz sushi rice
2 tbsp rice vinegar
4 tsp caster sugar
$\frac{1}{2}$ tsp salt
2 sheets sushi nori
60 g/2$\frac{1}{2}$ oz smoked salmon
$\frac{1}{4}$ cucumber, cut into fine strips

To serve:

wasabi
soy sauce
pickled ginger

Tasty tip

If wasabi is unavailable, use a little horseradish. If unable to get sushi nori (seaweed sheets), shape the rice into small bite-size oblongs, then drape a piece of smoked salmon over each one and garnish with chives.

2

3

4

Honey & Ginger Prawns

1 Cut the carrot into matchsticks, roughly chop the bamboo shoots and finely slice the spring onions.

2 Combine the bamboo shoots with the carrot matchsticks and spring onions.

3 In a wok or large frying pan, gently heat the honey, tomato ketchup, soy sauce, ginger, garlic and lime juice with 3 tablespoons of water. Bring to the boil.

4 Add the carrot mixture and stir-fry for 2–3 minutes until the vegetables are hot.

5 Add the prawns and continue to stir-fry for 2 minutes.

6 Remove the wok or frying pan from the heat and reserve until cooled slightly.

7 Divide the little gem lettuce into leaves and rinse lightly.

8 Stir the chopped coriander into the prawn mixture and season to taste with salt and pepper. Spoon into the lettuce leaves and serve immediately, garnished with sprigs of fresh coriander and lime slices.

Ingredients   SERVES 4

1 carrot
50 g/2 oz bamboo shoots
4 spring onions
1 tbsp clear honey
1 tbsp tomato ketchup
1 tsp soy sauce
2.5 cm/1 inch piece fresh root
    ginger, peeled and finely grated
1 garlic clove, peeled and crushed
1 tbsp lime juice
175 g/6 oz peeled prawns, thawed
    if frozen
2 heads little gem lettuce leaves
2 tbsp freshly chopped coriander
salt and freshly ground black pepper

To garnish:
fresh coriander sprigs
lime slices

Tuna Chowder

1 Heat the oil in a large heavy–based saucepan. Add the onion and celery and cook gently for about 5 minutes, stirring from time to time, until the onion is softened.

2 Stir in the flour and cook for about 1 minute to thicken.

3 Draw the pan off the heat and gradually pour in the milk, stirring throughout. Add the tuna and its liquid, the drained sweetcorn and the thyme. Mix gently, then bring to the boil. Cover and simmer for 5 minutes.

4 Remove the pan from the heat and season to taste with salt and pepper.

5 Sprinkle the chowder with the cayenne pepper and chopped parsley. Divide into soup bowls and serve immediately.

Ingredients   SERVES 4

2 tsp oil
1 onion, peeled and finely chopped
2 sticks of celery, trimmed and
   finely sliced
1 tbsp plain flour
600 ml/1 pint skimmed milk
200 g can tuna in water
320 g can sweetcorn in
   water, drained
2 tsp freshly chopped thyme
salt and freshly ground black pepper
pinch cayenne pepper
2 tbsp freshly chopped parsley

Tasty tip

To make this soup even more colourful replace the can of sweetcorn with a can of sweetcorn with peppers. For those who particularly like fish and seafood, add 125 g/4 oz of peeled prawns for extra flavour.

Oriental Minced Chicken on Rocket & Tomato

1 Finely chop the shallots and garlic. Cut the carrot into matchsticks, thinly slice the water chestnuts and reserve. Heat the oil in a wok or heavy-based large frying pan and add the chicken. Stir-fry for 3–4 minutes over a moderately high heat, breaking up any large pieces of chicken.

2 Add the garlic and shallots and cook for 2–3 minutes until softened. Sprinkle over the Chinese five-spice powder and the chilli powder and continue to cook for about 1 minute.

3 Add the carrot, water chestnuts, soy and fish sauce and 2 tablespoons of water. Stir-fry for a further 2 minutes. Remove from the heat and reserve to cool slightly.

4 Deseed the tomatoes and cut into thin wedges. Toss with the rocket and divide between four serving plates. Spoon the warm chicken mixture over the rocket and tomato wedges and serve immediately to prevent the rocket from wilting.

Ingredients　　　　SERVES 4

2 shallots, peeled
1 garlic clove, peeled
1 carrot, peeled
50 g/2 oz water chestnuts
1 tsp oil
350 g/12 oz fresh chicken mince
1 tsp Chinese five-spice powder
pinch chilli powder
1 tsp soy sauce
1 tbsp fish sauce
8 cherry tomatoes
50 g/2 oz rocket

Tasty tip

This is a very versatile dish. In place of the chicken you could use any lean cut of meat or even prawns. To make this dish a main meal, replace the rocket and tomatoes with stir-fried vegetables and rice.

Potato Pancakes

1. To make the sauce, mix together the crème fraîche, horseradish, lime rind and juice and chives. Cover and reserve.

2. Place the potatoes in a large saucepan and cover with lightly salted boiling water. Bring back to the boil, cover and simmer for 15 minutes, or until the potatoes are tender. Drain and mash until smooth. Cool for 5 minutes, then whisk in the egg white, milk, flour, thyme and salt to form a thick, smooth batter. Leave to stand for 30 minutes, then stir before using.

3. Heat a little oil in a heavy-based frying pan. Add 2–3 large spoonfuls of batter to make a small pancake and cook for 1–2 minutes until golden. Flip the pancake and cook for a further minute, or until golden. Repeat with the remaining batter to make 8 pancakes.

4. Arrange the pancakes on a plate and top with the smoked mackerel. Garnish with herbs and serve immediately with spoonfuls of the reserved horseradish sauce.

Ingredients   SERVES 6

For the sauce:
4 tbsp crème fraîche
1 tbsp horseradish sauce
juice and grated rind of 1 lime
1 tbsp freshly snipped chives

225 g/8 oz floury potatoes, peeled
   and cut into chunks
1 small egg white
2 tbsp milk
2 tsp self-raising flour
1 tbsp freshly chopped thyme
large pinch salt
a little vegetable oil, for frying
225 g/8 oz smoked mackerel fillets,
   skinned and roughly chopped
fresh herbs, to garnish

Helpful hint

Keep the pancakes warm as you make them by stacking on a warmed plate. Place greaseproof paper between each pancake to keep them separate and fold a clean tea towel loosely over the top.

Sweet Potato Crisps with Mango Salsa

1 To make the salsa, mix the mango with the tomatoes, cucumber and onion. Add the sugar, chilli, vinegar, oil and the lime rind and juice. Mix together thoroughly, cover and leave for 45–50 minutes.

2 Soak the potatoes in cold water for 40 minutes to remove as much of the excess starch as possible. Drain and dry thoroughly in a clean tea towel, or absorbent kitchen paper.

3 Heat the oil to 190°C/375°F in a deep fryer. When at the correct temperature, place half the potatoes in the frying basket, then carefully lower the potatoes into the hot oil and cook for 4–5 minutes, or until they are golden brown, shaking the basket every minute so that they do not stick together.

4 Drain the potato crisps on absorbent kitchen paper, sprinkle with sea salt and place under a preheated moderate grill for a few seconds to dry out. Repeat with the remaining potatoes. Stir the mint into the salsa and serve with the potato crisps.

Ingredients   SERVES 6

For the salsa:

1 large mango, peeled, stoned and
    cut into small cubes
8 cherry tomatoes, quartered
$^1/_2$ cucumber, peeled if preferred and
    finely diced
1 red onion, peeled and
    finely chopped
pinch of sugar
1 red chilli, deseeded and
    finely chopped
2 tbsp rice vinegar
2 tbsp olive oil
grated rind and juice of 1 lime

450 g/1 lb sweet potatoes, peeled
    and thinly sliced
vegetable oil, for deep frying
sea salt
2 tbsp freshly chopped mint

1

3

4

Stuffed Vine Leaves

1 Soak the rice in cold water for 30 minutes. If using fresh vine leaves, blanch 5–6 leaves at a time in salted boiling water for 1 minute. Rinse and drain. If using preserved vine leaves, soak in tepid water for at least 20 minutes, drain, rinse and pat dry with absorbent kitchen paper.

2 Mix the onion and leeks with the herbs and half the oil. Add the drained rice, mix and season to taste with salt and pepper. Stir in the currants, apricots, pine nuts and lemon juice. Spoon 1 teaspoon of the filling at the stalk end of each leaf. Roll, tucking the side flaps into the centre to create a neat parcel; do not roll too tight. Continue until all the filling is used.

3 Layer half the remaining vine leaves over the base of a large frying pan. Pack the little parcels in the frying pan and cover with the remaining leaves.

4 Pour in enough stock to just cover the vine leaves, add a pinch of salt and bring to the boil. Reduce the heat, cover and simmer for 45–55 minutes, or until the rice is sticky and tender. Leave to stand for 10 minutes. Drain the stock. Garnish with lemon wedges and serve hot with the Greek yogurt.

Ingredients   SERVES 6–8

150 g/5 oz long-grain rice
225 g/8 oz fresh or preserved
   vine leaves
225 g/8 oz red onion, peeled and
   finely chopped
3 baby leeks, trimmed and
   finely sliced
25 g/1 oz freshly chopped parsley
25 g/1 oz freshly chopped mint
25 g/1 oz freshly chopped dill
150 ml/$^1/_4$ pint extra virgin olive oil
salt and freshly ground black pepper
50 g/2 oz currants
50 g/2 oz ready-to-eat dried
   apricots, finely chopped
25 g/1 oz pine nuts
juice of 1 lemon
600–750 ml/1–1$^1/_4$ pints
   boiling stock
lemon wedges or slices, to garnish
4 tbsp Greek yogurt, to serve

2

2

3

Potato Skins

1. Preheat the oven to 200°C/400°F/Gas Mark 6. Scrub the potatoes, then prick a few times with a fork or skewer and place directly on the top shelf of the oven. Bake in the preheated oven for at least 1 hour, or until tender. The potatoes are cooked when they yield gently to the pressure of your hand.

2. Set the potatoes aside until cool enough to handle, then cut in half and scoop the flesh into a bowl and reserve. Preheat the grill and line the grill rack with foil.

3. Mix together the oil and the paprika and use half to brush the outside of the potato skins. Place on the grill rack under the preheated hot grill and cook for 5 minutes, or until crisp, turning as necessary.

4. Heat the remaining paprika-flavoured oil and gently fry the pancetta until crisp. Add to the potato flesh along with the cream, Gorgonzola cheese and parsley. Halve the potato skins and fill with the Gorgonzola filling. Return to the oven for a further 15 minutes to heat through. Sprinkle with a little more paprika and serve immediately with mayonnaise, sweet chilli sauce and a green salad.

Ingredients   SERVES 4

4 large baking potatoes
2 tbsp olive oil
2 tsp paprika
125 g/4 oz pancetta, roughly
    chopped
6 tbsp double cream
125 g/4 oz Gorgonzola cheese
1 tbsp freshly chopped parsley

To serve:

mayonnaise
sweet chilli dipping sauce
tossed green salad

Food fact

A popular, well-known Italian cheese, Gorgonzola was first made over 1,100 years ago in the village of the same name near Milan. Now mostly produced in Lombardy, it is made from pasteurised cows' milk and allowed to ripen for at least 3 months, giving it a rich but not overpowering flavour. Unlike most blue cheeses, it should have a greater concentration of veining towards the centre of the cheese.

Ginger & Garlic Potatoes

1 Scrub the potatoes, then place unpeeled in a large saucepan and cover with boiling salted water. Bring to the boil and cook for 15 minutes, then drain and leave the potatoes to cool completely. Peel and cut into 2.5 cm/1 inch cubes.

2 Place the root ginger, garlic, turmeric, salt and cayenne pepper in a food processor and blend for 1 minute. With the motor still running, slowly add 3 tablespoons of water and blend into a paste. Alternatively, pound the ingredients to a paste with a pestle and mortar.

3 Heat the oil in a large heavy-based frying pan and, when hot but not smoking, add the fennel seeds and fry for a few minutes. Stir in the ginger paste and cook for 2 minutes, stirring frequently. Take care not to burn the mixture.

4 Reduce the heat, then add the potatoes and cook for 5–7 minutes, stirring frequently, until the potatoes have a golden-brown crust. Add the diced apple and spring onions, then sprinkle with the freshly chopped coriander. Heat through for 2 minutes, then serve on assorted salad leaves with curry-flavoured mayonnaise.

Ingredients   SERVES 4

700 g/1$^1/_2$ lb potatoes
2.5 cm/1 inch piece of root ginger, peeled and coarsely chopped
3 garlic cloves, peeled and chopped
$^1/_2$ tsp turmeric
1 tsp salt
$^1/_2$ tsp cayenne pepper
5 tbsp vegetable oil
1 tsp whole fennel seeds
1 large eating apple, cored and diced
6 spring onions, trimmed and sliced diagonally
1 tbsp freshly chopped coriander

To serve:
assorted bitter salad leaves
curry-flavoured mayonnaise

Food fact
Turmeric comes from the same family as ginger. When the root is dried, it has a dull yellow appearance and can be ground to a powder that can be used in a wide range of savoury dishes. It has a warm spicy flavour, and gives food a wonderful golden colour.

Thai Crab Cakes

1 Put the rice in a large saucepan and add the hot stock. Bring to the boil, cover and simmer over a low heat without stirring for 18 minutes, or until the grains are tender and all the liquid is absorbed.

2 To make the cakes, place the crab meat, fish, spring onions, lemon grass, chilli, ginger, coriander, flour and egg in a food processor. Blend until all the ingredients are mixed thoroughly, then season to taste with salt and pepper. Add the rice to the processor and blend once more, but do not overmix.

3 Remove the mixture from the processor and place on a clean work surface. With damp hands, divide into 12 even-sized patties. Transfer to a plate, cover and chill in the refrigerator for about 30 minutes.

4 Heat the oil in a heavy-based frying pan and cook the crab cakes, four at a time, for 3–5 minutes on each side until crisp and golden. Drain on absorbent kitchen paper and serve immediately with a chilli dipping sauce.

Ingredients   SERVES 4

200 g/7 oz easy-cook basmati rice
450 ml/³/₄ pint chicken stock, heated
200 g/7 oz cooked crab meat
125 g/4 oz cod fillet, skinned
    and minced
5 spring onions, trimmed and
    finely chopped
1 lemon grass stalk, outer leaves
    discarded, and finely chopped
1 green chilli, deseeded and
    finely chopped
1 tbsp freshly grated root ginger
1 tbsp freshly chopped coriander
1 tbsp plain flour
1 medium egg
salt and freshly ground black pepper
2 tbsp vegetable oil, for frying

To serve:
sweet chilli dipping sauce
fresh salad leaves

Rice & Papaya Salad

1 Rinse and drain the rice and pour into a saucepan. Add 450 ml/³/₄ pint boiling salted water and the cinnamon stick. Bring to the boil, reduce the heat to very low, cover and cook without stirring for 15–18 minutes, or until all the liquid is absorbed. The rice should be light and fluffy and have steam holes on the surface. Remove the cinnamon stick and stir in the rind from 1 lime.

2 To make the dressing, place the bird's-eye chilli, remaining rind and lime and lemon juice, fish sauce and sugar in a food processor, and mix for a few minutes until blended. Alternatively, place all these ingredients in a screw-top jar and shake until well blended. Pour half the dressing over the hot rice and toss until the rice glistens.

3 Cut the papaya and mango into thin slices, then place in a bowl. Add the chopped green chilli, coriander and mint. Place the chicken on a chopping board, then remove and discard any skin or sinews. Cut into fine shreds and add to the bowl with the chopped peanuts.

4 Add the remaining dressing to the chicken mixture and stir until all the ingredients are lightly coated. Spoon the rice onto a platter, pile the chicken mixture on top and serve with warm strips of pitta bread.

Ingredients SERVES 4

175 g/6 oz easy-cook basmati rice
1 cinnamon stick, bruised
1 bird's-eye chilli, deseeded and
    finely chopped
rind and juice of 2 limes
rind and juice of 2 lemons
2 tbsp Thai fish sauce
1 tbsp soft light brown sugar
1 papaya, peeled and seeds removed
1 mango, peeled and stone removed
1 green chilli, deseeded and finely
    chopped
2 tbsp freshly chopped coriander
1 tbsp freshly chopped mint
250 g/9 oz cooked chicken
50 g/2 oz roasted peanuts, chopped
strips of pitta bread, to serve

Helpful hint

The papaya or pawpaw's skin turns from green when unripe, through to yellow and orange. To prepare, cut in half lengthways, scoop out the black seeds with a teaspoon and discard. Cut away the thin skin before slicing.

Moo Shi Pork

1 Cut the pork across the grain into 1 cm/¹/₂ inch slices, then cut into thin strips. Place in a bowl with the Chinese rice wine or sherry, soy sauce and cornflour. Mix well and reserve. Trim off the tough ends of the golden needles, then cut in half and reserve.

2 Heat a wok or large frying pan, add 1 tablespoon of the groundnut oil and, when hot, add the lightly beaten eggs and cook for 1 minute, stirring all the time, until scrambled. Remove and reserve. Wipe the wok clean with absorbent kitchen paper.

3 Return the wok to the heat, add the remaining oil and, when hot, transfer the pork strips from the marinade mixture to the wok, shaking off as much marinade as possible. Stir–fry for 30 seconds, then add the ginger, spring onions and bamboo shoots and pour in the marinade. Stir–fry for 2–3 minutes or until cooked.

4 Return the scrambled eggs to the wok, season to taste with salt and pepper and stir for a few seconds until mixed well and heated through. Divide the mixture between the pancakes, drizzle each with 1 teaspoon of hoisin sauce and roll up. Garnish and serve immediately.

Ingredients   SERVES 4

175 g/6 oz pork fillet
2 tsp Chinese rice wine or dry sherry
2 tbsp light soy sauce
1 tsp cornflour
25 g/1 oz dried golden needles,
   soaked and drained
2 tbsp groundnut oil
3 medium eggs, lightly beaten
1 tsp freshly grated root ginger
3 spring onions, trimmed and
   thinly sliced
150 g/5 oz bamboo shoots, cut into
   fine strips
salt and freshly ground black pepper
8 mandarin pancakes, steamed
hoisin sauce
sprigs of fresh coriander, to garnish

Helpful hint

Golden needles, also known as tiger lily buds, are dried, unopened lily flowers. They need to be soaked in hot water for about 30 minutes before use, then rinsed and squeezed dry. Omit them if you prefer and increase the quantity of pork to 225 g/8 oz.

Crispy Pork Wontons

1 Place the onion, garlic, chilli and ginger in a food processor and blend until very finely chopped. Add the pork, coriander and Chinese five-spice powder. Season to taste with salt and pepper, then blend again briefly to mix. Divide the mixture into 20 equal portions and, with floured hands, shape each into a walnut-sized ball.

2 Brush the edges of a wonton wrapper with beaten egg, place a pork ball in the centre, then bring the corners to the centre and pinch together to make a money bag. Repeat with the remaining pork balls and wrappers.

3 Pour sufficient oil into a heavy-based saucepan or deep-fat fryer so that it is one-third full and heat to 180°C/350°F. Deep-fry the wontons in three or four batches for 3–4 minutes, or until cooked through and golden and crisp. Drain on absorbent kitchen paper. Serve the crispy pork wontons immediately, allowing five per person, with some chilli sauce for dipping.

Ingredients   SERVES 4

1 small onion, peeled and roughly
   chopped
2 garlic cloves, peeled and crushed
1 green chilli, deseeded and chopped
2.5 cm/1 inch piece fresh root ginger,
   peeled and roughly chopped
450 g/1 lb lean pork mince
4 tbsp freshly chopped coriander
1 tsp Chinese five-spice powder
salt and freshly ground black pepper
20 wonton wrappers
1 medium egg, lightly beaten
vegetable oil, for deep-frying
chilli sauce, to serve

Tasty tip

When frying the wontons, use a deep, heavy-based saucepan or special deep-fat fryer. Never fill the pan more than one-third full with oil. To check the temperature, either use a cooking thermometer, or drop a cube of day-old bread into the hot oil. It will turn golden-brown in 45 seconds when the oil is hot enough.

Mixed Satay Sticks

1 Preheat the grill on high just before required. Soak eight bamboo skewers in cold water for at least 30 minutes. Peel the prawns, leaving the tails on. Using a sharp knife, remove the black vein along the back of the prawns. Cut the beef into 1 cm/^{1}/$_2$ inch wide strips. Place the prawns and beef in separate bowls and sprinkle each with ^{1}/$_2$ tablespoon of the lemon juice.

2 Mix together the garlic, pinch of salt, sugar, cumin, coriander, turmeric and groundnut oil to make a paste. Lightly brush over the prawns and beef. Cover and place in the refrigerator to marinate for at least 30 minutes, but for longer if possible.

3 Meanwhile, make the sauce. Pour 125 ml/4 fl oz of water into a small saucepan, add the shallot and sugar and heat gently until the sugar has dissolved. Stir in the creamed coconut and chilli powder. When melted, remove from the heat and stir in the peanut butter. Leave to cool slightly, then spoon into a serving dish.

4 Thread three prawns each on to four skewers and divide the sliced beef between the remaining skewers (see finished picture).

5 Cook the skewers under the preheated grill for 4–5 minutes, turning occasionally. The prawns should be opaque and pink and the beef browned on the outside, but still pink in the centre. Transfer to warmed individual serving plates, garnish with a few fresh coriander leaves and serve immediately with the warm peanut sauce.

Ingredients   SERVES 4

12 large raw prawns
350 g/12 oz beef rump steak
1 tbsp lemon juice
1 garlic clove, peeled and
    crushed
pinch of salt
2 tsp soft dark brown sugar
1 tsp ground cumin
1 tsp ground coriander
^{1}/$_4$ tsp ground turmeric
1 tbsp groundnut oil
fresh coriander leaves, to garnish

For the spicy peanut sauce:

1 shallot, peeled and very finely
    chopped
1 tsp demerara sugar
50 g/2 oz creamed coconut,
    chopped
pinch of chilli powder
1 tbsp dark soy sauce
125 g/4 oz crunchy peanut butter

Sweetcorn Fritters

1 Heat 1 tablespoon of the groundnut oil in a frying pan, add the onion and cook gently for 7–8 minutes or until beginning to soften. Add the chilli, garlic and ground coriander and cook for 1 minute, stirring continuously. Remove from the heat.

2 Drain the sweetcorn and tip into a mixing bowl. Lightly mash with a potato masher to break down the corn a little. Add the cooked onion mixture to the bowl with the spring onions and beaten egg. Season to taste with salt and pepper, then stir to mix together. Sift the flour and baking powder over the mixture and stir in.

3 Heat 2 tablespoons of the groundnut oil in a large frying pan. Drop 4 or 5 heaped teaspoonfuls of the sweetcorn mixture into the pan and, using a fish slice or spatula, flatten each to make a 1 cm/^{1}/$_2$ inch thick fritter.

4 Fry the fritters for 3 minutes, or until golden brown on the underside, turn over and fry for a further 3 minutes, or until cooked through and crisp.

5 Remove the fritters from the pan and drain on absorbent kitchen paper. Keep warm while cooking the remaining fritters, adding a little more oil if needed. Garnish with spring onion curls and serve immediately with a Thai-style chutney.

Ingredients   SERVES 4

4 tbsp groundnut oil
1 small onion, peeled and
    finely chopped
1 red chilli, deseeded and
    finely chopped
1 garlic clove, peeled and crushed
1 tsp ground coriander
325 g can sweetcorn
6 spring onions, trimmed and
    finely sliced
1 medium egg, lightly beaten
salt and freshly ground black pepper
3 tbsp plain flour
1 tsp baking powder
spring onion curls, to garnish
Thai-style chutney, to serve

Sesame Prawn Toasts

1 Place the prawns in a food processor or blender with the cornflour, spring onions, ginger, soy sauce and Chinese five–spice powder, if using. Blend to a fairly smooth paste. Spoon into a bowl and stir in the beaten egg. Season to taste with salt and pepper.

2 Cut the crusts off the bread. Spread the prawn paste in an even layer on one side of each slice. Sprinkle over the sesame seeds and press down lightly.

3 Cut each slice diagonally into four triangles. Place on a board and chill in the refrigerator for 30 minutes.

4 Pour sufficient oil into a heavy-based saucepan or deep-fat fryer so that it is one-third full. Heat until it reaches a temperature of 180°C/350°F. Cook the toasts in batches of five or six, carefully lowering them seeded-side down into the oil. Deep-fry for 2–3 minutes, or until lightly browned, then turn over and cook for 1 minute more. Using a slotted spoon, lift out the toasts and drain on absorbent kitchen paper. Keep warm while frying the remaining toasts. Arrange on a warmed platter and serve immediately with some chilli sauce for dipping.

Ingredients SERVES 4

125 g/4 oz peeled cooked prawns
1 tbsp cornflour
2 spring onions, peeled and
   roughly chopped
2 tsp freshly grated root ginger
2 tsp dark soy sauce
pinch of Chinese five–spice
   powder (optional)
1 small egg, beaten
salt and freshly ground black pepper
6 thin slices day-old white bread
40 g/1$^1/_2$ oz sesame seeds
vegetable oil for deep-frying
chilli sauce, to serve

Helpful hint

The toasts can be prepared to the end of step 3 up to 12 hours in advance. Cover and chill in the refrigerator until needed. It is important to use bread that is a day or two old and not fresh bread. Make sure that the prawns are well-drained before puréeing – pat them dry on absorbent kitchen paper, if necessary.

Sweet-&-Sour Battered Fish

1 Cut the fish into pieces about 5 x 2.5 cm/2 x 1 inch. Place 4 tablespoons of the flour in a small bowl, season with salt and pepper to taste, then add the fish strips a few at a time and toss until coated.

2 Sift the remaining flour into a bowl with a pinch of salt, the cornflour and arrowroot. Gradually whisk in 300 ml/^{1}/$_2$ pint ice-cold water to make a smooth, thin batter.

3 Heat the oil in a wok or deep-fat fryer to 190°C/375°F. Working in batches, dip the fish strips in the batter and deep-fry them for 3–5 minutes, or until crisp. Using a slotted spoon, remove the strips and drain on absorbent kitchen paper.

4 Meanwhile, make the sauce. Place 3 tablespoons of the orange juice, the vinegar, sherry, soy sauce, sugar, tomato purée and red pepper in a small saucepan. Bring to the boil, lower the heat and simmer for 3 minutes.

5 Blend the cornflour with the remaining orange juice, stir into the sauce and simmer, stirring, for 1 minute or until thickened. Arrange the fish on a warmed platter or individual plates. Drizzle a little of the sauce over and serve immediately with the remaining sauce.

Ingredients   SERVES 4–6

450 g/1 lb cod fillet, skinned
150 g/5 oz plain flour
salt and freshly ground black pepper
2 tbsp cornflour
2 tbsp arrowroot
vegetable oil, for deep-frying

For the sweet-&-sour sauce:

4 tbsp orange juice
2 tbsp white wine vinegar
2 tbsp dry sherry
1 tbsp dark soy sauce
1 tbsp soft light brown sugar
2 tsp tomato purée
1 red pepper, deseeded and diced
2 tsp cornflour

Tasty tip

Any firm white fish can be used for this dish, as long as it is fairly thick. Your fishmonger can tell you which varieties are suitable.

Spicy Beef Pancakes

1 Sift the flour, salt and Chinese five-spice powder into a bowl and make a well in the centre. Add the egg yolk and a little of the milk. Gradually beat in, drawing in the flour to make a smooth batter. Whisk in the rest of the milk.

2 Heat 1 teaspoon of the sunflower oil in a small heavy-based frying pan. Pour in just enough batter to thinly coat the base of the pan. Cook over a medium heat for 1 minute, or until the underside of the pancake is golden brown.

3 Turn or toss the pancake and cook for 1 minute, or until the other side of the pancake is golden brown. Make 7 more pancakes with the remaining batter. Stack them on a warmed plate as you make them, with greaseproof paper between each pancake. Cover with foil and keep warm in a low oven.

4 To make the filling, heat a wok or large frying pan, add the sesame oil and, when hot, add the spring onions, ginger and garlic and stir-fry for 1 minute. Add the beef strips, stir-fry for 3–4 minutes, then stir in the chilli, vinegar, sugar and soy sauce. Cook for 1 minute, then remove from the heat.

5 Spoon one eighth of the filling over one half of each pancake. Fold the pancakes in half, then fold in half again. Garnish with a few slices of spring onion and serve immediately.

Ingredients   SERVES 4

50 g/2 oz plain flour
pinch of salt
$1/2$ tsp Chinese five-spice powder
1 large egg yolk
150 ml/$1/4$ pint milk
4 tsp sunflower oil
slices of spring onion, to garnish

For the spicy beef filling:

1 tbsp sesame oil
4 spring onions, sliced
1 cm/$1/2$ inch piece fresh root ginger,
    peeled and grated
1 garlic clove, peeled and crushed
300 g/11 oz sirloin steak, trimmed
    and cut into strips
1 red chilli, deseeded and
    finely chopped
1 tsp sherry vinegar
1 tsp soft dark brown sugar
1 tbsp dark soy sauce

Lion's Head Pork Balls

1   Place the rice in a bowl and pour over plenty of cold water. Cover and soak for 2 hours. Tip into a sieve and drain well.

2   Place the pork, garlic, cornflour, Chinese five-spice powder, soy sauce, Chinese rice wine or sherry and coriander in a bowl. Season to taste with salt and pepper and mix together.

3   With slightly wet hands, shape the pork mixture into 20 walnut-sized balls, then roll in the rice to coat. Place the balls slightly apart in a steamer or a colander set over a saucepan of boiling water, cover and steam for 20 minutes, or until cooked through.

4   Meanwhile, make the dipping sauce. Stir together the sugar, vinegar and soy sauce until the sugar dissolves. Add the shallot, chilli and sesame oil and whisk together with a fork. Transfer to a small serving bowl, cover and leave to stand for at least 10 minutes before serving.

5   Remove the pork balls from the steamer and arrange them on a warmed serving platter. Serve immediately with the sweet chilli dipping sauce.

Ingredients
SERVES 4

75 g/3 oz glutinous rice
450 g/1 lb lean pork mince
2 garlic cloves, peeled and crushed
1 tbsp cornflour
$1/2$ tsp Chinese five-spice powder
2 tsp dark soy sauce
1 tbsp Chinese rice wine or dry sherry
2 tbsp freshly chopped coriander
salt and freshly ground black pepper

For the sweet chilli dipping sauce:

2 tsp caster sugar
1 tbsp sherry vinegar
1 tbsp light soy sauce
1 shallot, peeled and very
    finely chopped
1 small red chilli, deseeded and
    finely chopped
2 tsp sesame oil

Food fact

These meatballs get their name from the rice coating, which is thought to resemble a lion's mane.

1

3

4

Hot-&-Sour Squid

1 Slice open the body of each squid lengthways, open out and place on a chopping board with the inside uppermost. Using a sharp knife, score lightly in a criss-cross pattern. Cut each one into four pieces. Trim the tentacles.

2 Place the soy and hoisin sauces with the lime juice, sherry, honey, ginger, chillies and cornflour in a bowl. Season to taste with salt and pepper and mix together. Add the squid, stir well to coat, then cover and place in the refrigerator to marinate for 1 hour.

3 Tip the squid into a sieve over a small saucepan and strain off the marinade. Scrape any bits of chilli or ginger into the saucepan, as they will burn if fried.

4 Fill a deep-fat fryer one-third full with oil and heat to 180°C/350°F. Deep-fry the squid in batches for 2–3 minutes or until golden and crisp. Remove the squid and drain on absorbent kitchen paper. Keep warm.

5 Bring the marinade to the boil and let it bubble gently for a few seconds. Arrange the squid on a warmed serving dish and drizzle over the marinade. Garnish with lime wedges and serve immediately.

Ingredients   SERVES 4

8 baby squid, cleaned
2 tbsp dark soy sauce
2 tbsp hoisin sauce
1 tbsp lime juice
2 tbsp dry sherry
1 tbsp clear honey
2.5 cm/1 inch piece fresh root
    ginger, peeled and finely chopped
1 red chilli, deseeded and
    finely chopped
1 green chilli, deseeded and
    finely chopped
1 tsp cornflour
salt and freshly ground black pepper
vegetable oil, for deep-frying
lime wedges, to garnish

Helpful hint

It is simple to prepare squid. Rinse well in cold water, then firmly pull apart the head and body; the innards will come away with the head. Remove and discard the transparent beak. Rinse the body pouch thoroughly under cold running water and peel off the thin layer of dark skin.

1

2

4

Aromatic Quail Eggs

1 Place the tea leaves in a jug and pour over 150 ml/¹/₄ pint boiling water. Leave to stand for 5 minutes, then strain, reserving the tea and discarding the leaves.

2 Meanwhile, place the eggs in a saucepan with just enough cold water to cover them. Bring to the boil and simmer for 1 minute. Using a slotted spoon, move the eggs and roll them gently to just crack the shells all over.

3 Add the salt, 2 tablespoons of the soy sauce, dark brown sugar, star anise and cinnamon stick to the egg cooking water and pour in the tea. Bring to the boil, return the eggs to the saucepan and simmer for 1 minute. Remove from the heat and leave the eggs for 2 minutes, then remove the eggs and plunge them into cold water. Leave the tea mixture to cool.

4 Return the eggs to the cooled tea mixture, leave for 30 minutes, then drain and remove the shells to reveal the marbling.

5 Pour the remaining soy sauce, the vinegar and Chinese rice wine or sherry into a small saucepan and add the caster sugar and Chinese five-spice powder. Blend the cornflour with 1 tablespoon of cold water and stir into the soy sauce mixture. Heat until boiling and slightly thickened, stirring continuously. Leave to cool. Pour into a small serving dish. Place the eggs in a serving bowl or divide between individual plates and serve with the dipping sauce.

Ingredients   SERVES 6

2 tbsp jasmine tea leaves
24 quail eggs
2 tsp salt
4 tbsp dark soy sauce
1 tbsp soft dark brown sugar
2 whole star anise
1 cinnamon stick
2 tbsp sherry vinegar
2 tbsp Chinese rice wine or
    dry sherry
2 tbsp caster sugar
¹/₄ tsp Chinese five-spice powder
¹/₄ tsp cornflour

Tasty tip

This recipe can also be used to marble and flavour ordinary eggs. Allowing 9 eggs to serve 6 people, simmer for 4 minutes in step 2 and for a further 4 minutes in step 3. Leave the eggs to soak and peel as before, then cut widthways into quarters when serving.

Spicy Prawns in Lettuce Cups

1 Remove 3 or 4 of the tougher outer leaves of the lemon grass and reserve for another dish. Finely chop the remaining softer centre. Place 2 teaspoons of the chopped lemon grass in a bowl with the prawns, grated lime zest, chilli and ginger. Mix together to coat the prawns. Cover and place in the refrigerator to marinate while you make the coconut sauce.

2 For the sauce, place the grated coconut in a wok or non-stick frying pan and dry-fry for 2–3 minutes or until golden. Remove from the pan and reserve. Add the hoisin, soy and fish sauces to the pan with the sugar and 4 tablespoons of water. Simmer for 2–3 minutes, then remove from the heat. Leave to cool.

3 Pour the sauce over the prawns, add the toasted coconut and toss to mix together. Divide the prawn and coconut sauce mixture between the lettuce leaves and arrange on a platter.

4 Sprinkle over the chopped roasted peanuts and spring onions and garnish with a sprig of fresh coriander. Serve immediately.

Ingredients SERVES 4

1 lemon grass stalk
225 g/8 oz peeled cooked prawns
1 tsp finely grated lime zest
1 red bird's-eye chilli, deseeded and
   finely chopped
2.5 cm/1 inch piece fresh root
   ginger, peeled and grated
2 little gem lettuces, divided
   into leaves
25 g/1 oz roasted peanuts, chopped
2 spring onions, trimmed and
   diagonally sliced
sprig of fresh coriander, to garnish

For the coconut sauce:

2 tbsp freshly grated or unsweetened
   shredded coconut
1 tbsp hoisin sauce
1 tbsp light soy sauce
1 tbsp Thai fish sauce
1 tbsp palm sugar or soft light
   brown sugar

Cantonese Chicken Wings

1 Preheat the oven to 220°C/425°F/Gas Mark 7, 15 minutes before cooking. Place the hoisin sauce, soy sauce, sesame oil, garlic, ginger, Chinese rice wine or sherry, chilli bean sauce, vinegar and sugar in a small saucepan with 6 tablespoons of water. Bring to the boil, stirring occasionally, then simmer for about 30 seconds. Remove the glaze from the heat.

2 Place the chicken wings in a roasting tin in a single layer. Pour over the glaze and stir until the wings are coated thoroughly.

3 Cover the tin loosely with foil, place in the preheated oven and roast for 25 minutes. Remove the foil, baste the wings and cook for a further 5 minutes.

4 Reduce the oven temperature to 190°C/375°F/Gas Mark 5. Turn the wings over and sprinkle with the chopped cashew nuts and spring onions. Return to the oven and cook for 5 minutes, or until the nuts are lightly browned, the glaze is sticky and the wings are tender. Remove from the oven and leave to stand for 5 minutes before arranging on a warmed platter. Serve immediately with finger bowls and plenty of napkins.

Ingredients   SERVES 4

3 tbsp hoisin sauce
2 tbsp dark soy sauce
1 tbsp sesame oil
1 garlic clove, peeled and crushed
2.5 cm/1 inch piece fresh root
    ginger, peeled and grated
1 tbsp Chinese rice wine or dry sherry
2 tsp chilli bean sauce
2 tsp red or white wine vinegar
2 tbsp soft light brown sugar
900 g/2 lb large chicken wings
50 g/2 oz cashew nuts, chopped
2 spring onions, trimmed and
    finely chopped

Helpful hint

Chicken wings are regarded as a delicacy in both China and Thailand and are considered one of the tastiest parts of the bird. If you give your butcher advance notice, he will probably sell them to you very cheaply, as they are often trimmed off and discarded when cutting chickens into portions.

Vegetable Thai Spring Rolls

1 Place the vermicelli in a bowl and cover with boiling water. Leave to soak for 5 minutes or until softened, then drain. Cut into 7.5 cm/3 inch lengths. Soak the mushrooms in almost–boiling water for 15 minutes, drain, discard the stalks and slice thinly.

2 Heat a wok or large frying pan, add the groundnut oil and, when hot, add the carrots and stir–fry for 1 minute. Add the mangetout and spring onions and stir–fry for 2–3 minutes or until tender. Tip the vegetables into a bowl and leave to cool. Stir the vermicelli and shiitake mushrooms into the cooled vegetables with the bamboo shoots, ginger, soy sauce and egg yolk. Season to taste with salt and pepper and mix thoroughly.

3 Brush the edges of a spring roll wrapper with a little beaten egg white. Spoon 2 teaspoons of the vegetable filling on to the wrapper, in a 7.5 cm/3 inch log shape 2.5 cm/1 inch from one edge. Fold the wrapper edge over the filling, then fold in the right and left sides. Brush the folded edges with more egg white and roll up neatly. Place on an oiled baking sheet seam–side down and make the rest of the spring rolls.

4 Heat the oil in a heavy–based saucepan or deep-fat fryer to 180°C/350°F. Deep-fry the spring rolls six at a time for 2–3 minutes, or until golden brown and crisp. Drain on absorbent kitchen paper and arrange on a warmed platter. Garnish with spring onion tassels and serve immediately.

Ingredients   SERVES 4

50 g/2 oz cellophane vermicelli
4 dried shiitake mushrooms
1 tbsp groundnut oil
2 medium carrots, peeled and cut
    into fine matchsticks
125 g/4 oz mangetout, cut
    lengthways into fine strips
3 spring onions, trimmed and
    chopped
125 g/4 oz canned bamboo shoots,
    cut into fine matchsticks
1 cm/$\frac{1}{2}$ inch piece fresh root ginger,
    peeled and grated
1 tbsp light soy sauce
1 medium egg, separated
salt and freshly ground black pepper
20 spring roll wrappers, each about
    12.5 cm/5 inch square
vegetable oil for deep-frying
spring onion tassels, to garnish

1

2

3

Crispy Prawns with Chinese Dipping Sauce

1 Using a sharp knife, remove the black vein along the back of the prawns. Sprinkle the prawns with the salt and leave to stand for 15 minutes. Pat dry on absorbent kitchen paper.

2 Heat a wok or large frying pan, add the groundnut oil and, when hot, add the prawns and stir-fry in two batches for about 1 minute, or until they turn pink and are almost cooked. Using a slotted spoon, remove the prawns and keep warm in a low oven.

3 Drain the oil from the wok, leaving 1 tablespoon. Add the garlic, ginger and chilli and cook for about 30 seconds. Add the coriander, return the prawns and stir-fry for 1–2 minutes, or until the prawns are cooked through and the garlic is golden. Turn into a warmed serving dish.

4 For the dipping sauce, using a fork, beat together the soy sauce, rice wine vinegar, caster sugar and chilli oil in a small bowl. Stir in the spring onions. Serve immediately with the hot prawns.

Ingredients SERVES 4

450 g/1 lb medium-sized raw
  prawns, peeled
$^1/_4$ tsp salt
6 tbsp groundnut oil
2 garlic cloves, peeled and
  finely chopped
2.5 cm/1 inch piece fresh root
  ginger, peeled and finely chopped
1 green chilli, deseeded and
  finely chopped
4 stems fresh coriander, leaves and
  stems roughly chopped

For the Chinese dipping sauce:

3 tbsp dark soy sauce
3 tbsp rice wine vinegar
1 tbsp caster sugar
2 tbsp chilli oil
2 spring onions, finely shredded

Poached Fish Dumplings with Creamy Chilli Sauce

1 Chop the fish into chunks and place in a food processor with the soy sauce, cornflour and egg yolk. Season to taste with salt and pepper. Blend until fairly smooth. Add the coriander and process for a few seconds until well mixed. Transfer to a bowl, cover and chill in the refrigerator for 30 minutes.

2 With damp hands, shape the chilled mixture into walnut–sized balls and place on a baking tray lined with non–stick baking paper. Chill in the refrigerator for a further 30 minutes.

3 Pour the stock into a wide saucepan, bring to the boil, then reduce the heat until barely simmering. Add the fish balls and poach for 3–4 minutes or until cooked through.

4 Meanwhile, make the sauce. Heat the oil in a small saucepan, add the garlic and spring onions and cook until golden. Stir in the sherry, chilli and soy sauces and lemon juice, then remove immediately from the heat. Stir in the crème fraîche and season to taste with salt and pepper.

5 Using a slotted spoon, lift the cooked fish balls from the stock and place on a warmed serving dish. Drizzle over the sauce, garnish with sprigs of fresh coriander and serve immediately.

Ingredients   SERVES 4

450 g/1 lb white fish fillet, skinned
  and boned
1 tsp dark soy sauce
1 tbsp cornflour
1 medium egg yolk
salt and freshly ground black pepper
3 tbsp freshly chopped coriander, plus
  extra to garnish
1.6 litres/2^3/$_4$ pints fish stock

For the creamy chilli sauce:

2 tsp groundnut oil
2 garlic cloves, peeled and
  finely chopped
4 spring onions, trimmed and finely sliced
2 tbsp dry sherry
1 tbsp sweet chilli sauce
1 tbsp light soy sauce
1 tbsp lemon juice
6 tbsp crème fraîche

To garnish:

sprigs of fresh coriander
fresh carrot sticks

Wok-fried Snacks – Popcorn & Sesame-coated Pecans

1 For the popcorn, heat half the oil in a large wok over a medium–high heat. Add 2–3 kernels and cover with a lid. When these kernels pop, add all the popcorn and cover tightly. Cook until the popping stops, shaking from time to time. When the popping stops, pour the popped corn into a bowl and immediately add the remaining oil to the wok with the garlic salt and chilli powder. Stir–fry for 30 seconds, or until blended and fragrant. Return the popcorn to the wok, stir–fry and toss for a further 30 seconds, or until coated. Pour into the bowl and serve warm or at room temperature.

2 For the pecans, put the sugar, cinnamon, Chinese five–spice powder, salt and cayenne pepper into a large wok and stir in 50 ml/2 fl oz water. Bring to the boil over a high heat, then simmer for 4 minutes, stirring frequently.

3 Remove from the heat and stir in the pecans or walnuts until well coated. Turn on to a lightly oiled, non–stick baking sheet and sprinkle generously with the sesame seeds.

4 Working quickly with two forks, separate the nuts into individual pieces or bite–sized clusters. Sprinkle with a few more sesame seeds and leave to cool completely. Carefully remove from the baking sheet, breaking into smaller pieces if necessary.

Ingredients   SERVES 4–6

For the popcorn:

75 ml/ 3 fl oz vegetable oil
75 g/3 oz unpopped popcorn
$1/2$ tsp garlic salt
1 tsp hot chilli powder

For the pecans:

50 g/2 oz sugar
$1/2$ tsp ground cinnamon
$1/2$ tsp ground Chinese five–spice powder
$1/4$ tsp salt
$1/4$ tsp cayenne pepper
175 g/6 oz pecan or walnut halves
sesame seeds for sprinkling

Helpful hint

Popping corn is readily available and should be stored in an airtight container.

Prawn Toasts

1 Put the prawns, egg white, spring onions, ginger, garlic, cornflour, hot pepper sauce and sugar into a food processor. Season to taste with about $^1/_2$ teaspoon of salt and black pepper.

2 Process until the mixture forms a smooth paste, scraping down the side of the bowl once or twice.

3 Using a metal palette knife, spread an even layer of the paste evenly over the bread slices. Sprinkle each slice generously with sesame seeds, pressing gently to bury them in the paste.

4 Trim the crusts off each slice, then cut each slice diagonally into four triangles. Cut each triangle in half again to make eight pieces from each slice.

5 Heat the vegetable oil in a large wok to 190°C/375°F, or until a small cube of bread browns in about 30 seconds. Working in batches, fry the prawn triangles for 30–60 seconds, or until they are golden, turning once.

6 Remove with a slotted spoon and drain on absorbent kitchen paper. Keep the toasts warm. Arrange them on a large serving plate and garnish with sprigs of fresh coriander. Serve immediately.

Ingredients   SERVES 8–10

225 g/8 oz cooked peeled prawns, thawed if frozen, well drained and dried
1 medium egg white
2 spring onions, trimmed and chopped
1 cm/$^1/_2$ inch piece fresh root ginger, peeled and chopped
1 garlic clove, peeled and chopped
1 tsp cornflour
2–3 dashes hot pepper sauce
$^1/_2$ tsp sugar
salt and freshly ground black pepper
8 slices firm-textured white bread
4–5 tbsp sesame seeds
300 ml/$^1/_2$ pint vegetable oil for deep-frying
sprigs of fresh coriander, to garnish

Tasty tip
This is a classic Chinese appetiser. Serve it with a selection of other snacks as a starter, or with drinks.

Sesame Prawns

1 Remove the heads from the prawns by twisting away from the body and discard. Peel the prawns, leaving the tails on for presentation. Using a sharp knife, remove the black vein from the back of the prawns. Rinse and dry. Slice along the back, but do not cut through the prawn body. Place on the chopping board and press firmly to flatten slightly, to make a butterfly shape.

2 Put the flour, half the sesame seeds, salt and pepper into a food processor and blend for 30 seconds. Tip into a polythene bag and add the prawns, 4–5 at a time. Twist to seal, then shake to coat with the flour.

3 Beat the egg in a small bowl with the remaining sesame seeds, salt and pepper.

4 Heat the oil in a large wok to 190°C/375°F, or until a small cube of bread browns in about 30 seconds. Working in batches of five or six, and holding each prawn by the tail, dip into the beaten egg, then carefully lower into the oil. Cook for 1–2 minutes, or until crisp and golden, turning once or twice. Using a slotted spoon, remove the prawns, drain on absorbent kitchen paper and keep warm.

5 To make the sauce, stir together the soy sauce, spring onion, chillies, oil and sugar until the sugar dissolves. Arrange the prawns on a plate, garnish with spring onion and serve immediately.

Ingredients   SERVES 6–8

24 large raw prawns
40 g/1 oz plain flour
4 tbsp sesame seeds
salt and freshly ground black pepper
1 large egg
300 ml/^{1}/$_2$ pint vegetable oil, for
  deep-frying

For the soy dipping sauce:

50 ml/2 fl oz soy sauce
1 spring onion, trimmed and
  finely chopped
^{1}/$_2$ tsp dried crushed chillies
1 tbsp sesame oil
1–2 tsp sugar, or to taste
strips of spring onion, to garnish

Helpful hint

Raw prawns are widely available but are cheapest bought frozen in boxes from Asian and Chinese grocers.

Spring Rolls

1 Soak the Chinese mushrooms in almost–boiling water for 20 minutes. Remove and squeeze out the liquid. Discard any stems, slice and reserve. Soak the rice vermicelli as packet instructions.

2 Heat a large wok and, when hot, add the oil. Heat then add the onion, garlic and ginger and stir–fry for 2 minutes. Add the pork, spring onions and Chinese mushrooms and stir–fry for 4 minutes. Stir in the bean sprouts, water chestnuts, chives, prawns, oyster and soy sauces. Season to taste with salt and pepper and spoon into a bowl.

3 Drain the noodles well, add to the bowl and toss until well mixed, then leave to cool.

4 Blend the flour to a smooth paste with 3–4 tablespoons of water. Soften a wrapper in a plate of warm water for 1–2 seconds, then drain. Put 2 tablespoons of the filling near one edge of the wrapper, fold the edge over the filling, then fold in each side and roll up. Seal with a little flour paste and transfer to a baking sheet, seam–side down. Repeat with the remaining wrappers.

5 Heat the oil in a large wok to 190°C/375°F, or until a cube of bread browns in 30 seconds. Fry the spring rolls a few at a time, until golden. Remove and drain on absorbent kitchen paper. Arrange on a serving plate and garnish with spring onion tassels. Serve immediately.

Ingredients   MAKES 20–30 ROLLS

For the filling:

15 g/½ oz dried Chinese (shiitake) mushrooms
50 g/2 oz rice vermicelli
1–2 tbsp groundnut oil
1 small onion, peeled and finely chopped
3–4 garlic cloves, peeled, finely chopped
4 cm/1½ inch piece fresh root ginger, peeled and chopped
225 g/8 oz fresh pork mince
2 spring onions, trimmed, finely chopped
75 g/3 oz bean sprouts
4 water chestnuts, chopped
2 tbsp freshly snipped chives
175 g/6 oz cooked peeled prawns, chopped
1 tsp oyster sauce; 1 tsp soy sauce
salt and freshly ground black pepper
spring onion tassels, to garnish

For the wrappers:

4–5 tbsp plain flour
26–30 spring roll wrappers
300 ml/½ pint vegetable oil for deep-frying

Barbecue Pork Steamed Buns

1 Put 75 g/3 oz of the flour in a bowl and stir in the yeast. Heat the milk, oil, sugar and salt in a small saucepan until warm, stirring until the sugar has dissolved. Pour into the bowl and, with an electric mixer, beat on a low speed for 30 seconds, until blended. Beat at high speed for 3 minutes then, with a wooden spoon, stir in as much of the remaining flour as possible, until a stiff dough forms. Shape into a ball, place in a lightly oiled bowl, cover with clingfilm and leave for 1 hour in a warm place, or until doubled in size.

2 To make the filling, heat a wok, add the oil and, when hot, add the red pepper and garlic. Stir-fry for 4–5 minutes. Add the remaining ingredients and bring to the boil, stir-frying for 2–3 minutes until thick and syrupy. Cool and reserve.

3 Punch down the dough and turn onto a lightly floured surface. Divide into 12 pieces and shape them into balls, then cover and leave to rest for 5 minutes. Roll each ball to a 7.5 cm/3 inch circle. Place a heaped tablespoon of filling in the centre of each. Dampen the edges, then bring them up and around the filling, pinching together to seal. Place seam-side down on a small square of non-stick baking parchment. Continue with the remaining dough and filling. Leave to rise for 10 minutes. Bring a large wok half-filled with water to the boil, place the buns in a lightly oiled Chinese steamer, without touching each other. Cover and steam for 20–25 minutes, then remove and cool slightly. Garnish with spring onion tassels and serve with salad leaves.

Ingredients   SERVES 12

For the buns:

175–200 g/6–7 oz plain flour
1 tbsp dried yeast
125 ml/4 fl oz milk
2 tbsp sunflower oil
1 tbsp sugar
1/2 tsp salt
spring onion tassels, to garnish
fresh green salad leaves, to serve

For the filling:

2 tbsp vegetable oil
1 small red pepper, deseeded and
    finely chopped
2 garlic cloves, peeled and
    finely chopped
225 g/8 oz cooked pork,
    finely chopped
50 g/2 oz light brown sugar
50 ml/2 fl oz tomato ketchup
1–2 tsp hot chilli powder, or to taste

Chicken-filled Spring Rolls

1 Heat a large wok, add the oil and, when hot, add the diced bacon and stir-fry for 2–3 minutes, or until golden. Add the chicken and pepper and stir-fry for a further 2–3 minutes. Add the remaining filling ingredients and stir-fry for 3–4 minutes until all the vegetables are tender. Turn into a colander and leave to drain as the mixture cools completely.

2 Blend the flour with about 1½ tablespoons of water to form a paste. Soften each wrapper in a plate of warm water for 1–2 seconds, then place on a chopping board. Put 2–3 tablespoons of filling on the near edge. Fold the edge over the filling to cover. Fold in each side and roll up. Seal the edge with a little flour paste and press to seal securely. Transfer to a baking sheet, seam-side down.

3 Heat the oil in a large wok to 190°C/375°F, or until a small cube of bread browns in about 30 seconds. Working in batches of 3–4, fry the spring rolls until they are crisp and golden, turning once (about 2 minutes). Remove and drain on absorbent kitchen paper. Arrange the spring rolls on a serving plate, garnish with spring onion tassels and serve hot with dipping sauce.

Ingredients

MAKES
12–14 ROLLS

For the filling:

1 tbsp vegetable oil
2 slices streaky bacon, diced
225 g/8 oz skinless chicken breast
    fillets, thinly sliced
1 small red pepper, deseeded and
    finely chopped
4 spring onions, trimmed and
    finely chopped
2.5 cm/1 inch piece fresh root ginger,
    peeled and finely chopped
75 g/3 oz mangetout, thinly sliced
75 g/3 oz bean sprouts
1 tbsp soy sauce
2 tsp Chinese rice wine or dry sherry
2 tsp hoisin or plum sauce

For the wrappers:

3 tbsp plain flour
12–14 spring roll wrappers
300 ml/½ pint vegetable oil, for
    deep-frying
shredded spring onions, to garnish
dipping sauce, to serve

1

2

3

Fried Pork-filled Wontons

1 Place all the filling ingredients into a food processor and, using the pulse button, process until well blended. Do not overwork, the filling should have a coarse texture.

2 Lay out the wonton wrappers on a clean chopping board and put a teaspoon of the filling in the centre of each.

3 Brush the edges with a little water and bring up two opposite corners of each square over the filling to form a triangle, pressing the edges firmly to seal. Dampen the two other corners and overlap them slightly, pressing firmly to seal, to form an oven–envelope shape, similar to a tortellini.

4 For the dipping sauce, stir together all the sauce ingredients until the sugar is dissolved. Pour into a serving bowl and reserve.

5 Heat the oil in a large wok to 190°C/375°F, or until a small cube of bread browns in about 30 seconds.

6 Working in batches of 5–6, fry until the wontons are crisp and golden, turning once or twice. Remove and drain on absorbent kitchen paper. Garnish with spring onion tassels and serve hot with the dipping sauce.

Ingredients   MAKES 24

For the filling:

275 g/10 oz cooked pork, finely chopped
2–3 spring onions, trimmed and
　finely chopped
2.5 cm/1 inch piece root ginger, grated
1 garlic clove, peeled and crushed
1 small egg, lightly beaten
1 tbsp soy sauce
1 tsp soft light brown sugar
1 tsp sweet chilli sauce or ketchup
24–30 wonton wrappers, 8 cm/3$\frac{1}{2}$
　inches square
300 ml/$\frac{1}{2}$ pint vegetable oil, for
　deep–frying

For the ginger dipping sauce:

4 tbsp soy sauce
1–2 tbsp rice or raspberry vinegar
2.5 cm/1 inch piece fresh root ginger,
　peeled and finely slivered
1 tbsp sesame oil
1 tbsp soft light brown sugar
2–3 dashes hot chilli sauce
spring onion tassels, to garnish

Prawn Salad with Toasted Rice

1 Place all the ingredients for the dressing in a small bowl and leave to stand to let the flavours blend together.

2 Using a sharp knife, split each prawn lengthways in half, leaving the tail attached to one half. Remove the black vein and pat the prawns dry with absorbent kitchen paper. Sprinkle the prawns with a little salt and cayenne pepper and then reserve.

3 Heat a wok over a high heat. Add the rice and stir–fry until browned and fragrant. Turn into a mortar and cool. Crush gently with a pestle until coarse crumbs form. Wipe the wok clean.

4 Reheat the wok, add the oil and, when hot, add the prawns and stir–fry for 2 minutes, or until pink. Transfer to a plate and season to taste with salt and pepper.

5 Place the Chinese leaves or lettuce into a salad bowl with the cucumber, chives and mint leaves and toss lightly together.

6 Remove the lemon grass stalk and some of the chilli from the dressing and pour all but 2 tablespoons over the salad and toss until lightly coated. Add the prawns and drizzle with the remaining dressing, then sprinkle with the toasted rice and serve.

Ingredients   SERVES 4

For the dressing:
50 ml/2 fl oz rice vinegar
1 red chilli, deseeded and
    thinly sliced
7.5 cm/3 inch piece lemon grass
    stalk, bruised
juice of 1 lime
2 tbsp Thai fish sauce
1 tsp sugar, or to taste

For the salad:
350 g/12 oz large raw prawns, peeled
    with tails attached, heads removed
cayenne pepper
1 tbsp long–grain white rice
salt and freshly ground black pepper
2 tbsp sunflower oil
1 large head Chinese leaves or cos
    lettuce, shredded
1/2 small cucumber, peeled, deseeded
    and thinly sliced
1 small bunch chives, cut into 2.5
    cm/1 inch pieces
small bunch of mint leaves

Sticky Braised Spare Ribs

1 Put the spare ribs in a wok and add enough cold water to cover. Bring to the boil over a medium–high heat, skimming any scum that rises to the surface. Cover and simmer for 30 minutes, then drain and rinse the ribs.

2 Rinse and dry the wok and return the ribs to it. In a bowl, blend the apricot nectar or orange juice with the white wine, black bean sauce, tomato ketchup and honey until smooth.

3 Stir in the spring onions, garlic cloves and grated orange zest. Stir well until mixed thoroughly.

4 Pour the mixture over the spare ribs in the wok and stir gently until the ribs are lightly coated. Place over a moderate heat and bring to the boil.

5 Cover then simmer, stirring occasionally, for 1 hour, or until the ribs are tender and the sauce is thickened and sticky. If the sauce reduces too quickly or begins to stick, add water 1 tablespoon at a time until the ribs are tender. Adjust the seasoning to taste, then transfer the ribs to a serving plate and garnish with spring onion tassels and lemon wedges. Serve immediately.

Ingredients SERVES 4

900 g/2 lb meaty pork spare ribs, cut crossways into 7.5 cm/3 inch pieces

125 ml/4 fl oz apricot nectar or orange juice

50 ml/2 fl oz dry white wine

3 tbsp black bean sauce

3 tbsp tomato ketchup

2 tbsp clear honey

3–4 spring onions, trimmed and chopped

2 garlic cloves, peeled and crushed

grated zest of 1 small orange

salt and freshly ground black pepper

To garnish:

spring onion tassels

lemon wedges

Helpful hint

It's probably best to get your butcher to cut the ribs into pieces for you, as they are quite bony. Boiling the ribs before cooking them in the sauce reduces the fat content and ensures that they are tender and more succulent.

Soy-glazed Chicken Thighs

1 Heat a large wok and, when hot, add the oil and heat. Stir–fry the chicken thighs for 5 minutes or until golden. Remove and drain on absorbent kitchen paper. You may need to do this in 2–3 batches.

2 Pour off the oil and fat and, using absorbent kitchen paper, carefully wipe out the wok. Add the garlic, with the root ginger, soy sauce, Chinese rice wine or sherry and honey to the wok and stir well. Sprinkle in the soft brown sugar with the hot chilli sauce to taste, then place over the heat and bring to the boil.

3 Reduce the heat to a gentle simmer, then carefully add the chicken thighs. Cover the wok and simmer gently over a very low heat for 30 minutes, or until they are tender and the sauce is reduced and thickened and glazes the chicken thighs.

4 Stir or spoon the sauce occasionally over the chicken thighs and add a little water if the sauce is starting to become too thick. Arrange in a shallow serving dish, garnish with freshly chopped parsley and serve immediately.

Ingredients   SERVES 6–8

900 g/2 lb chicken thighs
2 tbsp vegetable oil
3–4 garlic cloves, peeled and crushed
4 cm/1$\frac{1}{2}$ inch piece fresh root
    ginger, peeled and finely chopped
    or grated
125 ml/4 fl oz soy sauce
2–3 tbsp Chinese rice wine or
    dry sherry
2 tbsp clear honey
1 tbsp soft brown sugar
2–3 dashes hot chilli sauce,
    or to taste
freshly chopped parsley, to garnish

Tasty tip

Often overlooked, chicken wings are inexpensive and very flavourful. Served this way, with a sticky coating, they make an ideal snack. Serve with finger bowls to clean sticky fingers.

Shredded Duck in Lettuce Leaves

1 Cover the dried Chinese mushrooms with almost–boiling water, leave for 20 minutes, then drain and slice thinly.

2 Heat a large wok, add the oil and, when hot, stir–fry the duck for 3–4 minutes, or until sealed. Remove with a slotted spoon and reserve.

3 Add the chilli, spring onions, garlic and Chinese mushrooms to the wok and stir–fry for 2–3 minutes, or until softened.

4 Add the bean sprouts, soy sauce, Chinese rice wine or dry sherry and honey or brown sugar to the wok and continue to stir–fry for 1 minute, or until blended.

5 Stir in the reserved duck and stir–fry for 2 minutes, or until well mixed together and heated right through. Transfer to a heated serving dish.

6 Arrange the hoisin sauce in a small bowl on a tray or plate with a pile of lettuce leaves and the mint leaves.

7 Let each guest spoon a little hoisin sauce onto a lettuce leaf, then top with a large spoonful of the stir–fried duck and vegetables and roll up the leaf to enclose the filling. Serve with the dipping sauce.

Ingredients SERVES 4–6

15 g/¹/₂ oz dried Chinese (shiitake)
    mushrooms
2 tbsp vegetable oil
400 g/14 oz boneless, skinless duck
    breast, cut crossways into thin strips
1 red chilli, deseeded and thinly
    sliced diagonally
4–6 spring onions, trimmed and
    diagonally sliced
2 garlic cloves, peeled and crushed
75 g/3 oz bean sprouts
3 tbsp soy sauce
1 tbsp Chinese rice wine or dry sherry
1–2 tsp clear honey or brown sugar
4–6 tbsp hoisin sauce
large, crisp lettuce leaves such as
    iceberg or cos
handful of fresh mint leaves
dipping sauce (see Sesame Prawns,
    page 160)

Food fact

Hoisin sauce is a sweet and spicy aromatic Chinese sauce made primarily from soy beans, sugar, garlic and chilli.

Swedish Cocktail Meatballs

1 Heat half the butter in a large wok, add the onion and cook, stirring frequently, for 4–6 minutes, or until softened and beginning to colour. Transfer to a bowl and leave to cool. Wipe out the wok with absorbent kitchen paper. Add the breadcrumbs and beaten egg with 1–2 tablespoons of cream to the softened onion. Season to taste with salt and pepper and stir until well blended. Using your fingertips, crumble the beef and pork mince into the bowl. Add half the dill, the allspice and, using your hands, mix together until well blended. With dampened hands, shape the mixture into 2.5 cm/1 inch balls.

2 Melt the remaining butter in the wok and add the vegetable oil, swirling it to coat the side of the wok. Working in batches, add about one quarter to one third of the meatballs in a single layer and cook for 5 minutes, swirling and turning until golden and cooked. Transfer to a plate and continue with the remaining meatballs, transferring them to the plate as they are cooked.

3 Pour off the fat in the wok. Add the beef stock and bring to the boil, then boil until reduced by half, stirring and scraping up any browned bits from the bottom. Add the remaining cream and continue to simmer until slightly thickened and reduced. Stir in the remaining dill and season if necessary. Add the meatballs and simmer for 2–3 minutes, or until heated right through. Serve with cocktail sticks, with the sauce in a separate bowl for dipping.

Ingredients SERVES 4–6

50 g/2 oz butter
1 onion, peeled and finely chopped
50 g/2 oz fresh white breadcrumbs
1 medium egg, beaten
125 ml/4 fl oz double cream
salt and freshly ground black pepper
350 g/12 oz fresh lean beef mince
125 g/4 oz fresh pork mince
3–4 tbsp freshly chopped dill
$^{1}/_{2}$ tsp ground allspice
1 tbsp vegetable oil
125 ml/4 fl oz beef stock
cream cheese and chive or cranberry
   sauce, to serve

Chicken & Lamb Satay

1 Preheat the grill just before cooking. Soak the bamboo skewers for 30 minutes before required. Cut the chicken and lamb into thin strips, about 7.5 cm/3 inches long and place in two shallow dishes. Blend all the marinade ingredients together, then pour half over the chicken and half over the lamb. Stir until lightly coated, then cover with clingfilm and leave to marinate in the refrigerator for at least 2 hours, turning occasionally.

2 Remove the chicken and lamb from the marinade and thread on to the skewers. Reserve the marinade. Cook under the preheated grill for 8–10 minutes or until cooked, turning and brushing with the marinade.

3 Meanwhile, make the peanut sauce. Blend the coconut milk with the peanut butter, fish sauce, lime juice, chilli powder and sugar. Pour into a saucepan and cook gently for 5 minutes, stirring occasionally, then season to taste with salt and pepper. Garnish with coriander sprigs and lime wedges and serve the satays with the prepared sauce.

Ingredients   MAKES 16

225 g/8 oz skinless, boneless chicken
225 g/8 oz lean lamb

For the marinade:

1 small onion, peeled and finely
   chopped
2 garlic cloves, peeled and crushed
2.5 cm/1 inch piece fresh root
   ginger, peeled and grated
4 tbsp soy sauce
1 tsp ground coriander
2 tsp dark brown sugar
2 tbsp lime juice; 1 tbsp vegetable oil

For the peanut sauce:

300 ml/$\frac{1}{2}$ pint coconut milk
4 tbsp crunchy peanut butter
1 tbsp Thai fish sauce
1 tsp lime juice; 1 tbsp chilli powder
1 tbsp brown sugar
salt and freshly ground black pepper

To garnish:

sprigs of fresh coriander
lime wedges

Sweetcorn Cakes

1   Place the flour in a bowl, make a well in the centre, then add the curry paste, soy sauce and the sugar together with the shredded kaffir lime leaves, French beans and sweetcorn. Season to taste with salt and pepper, then beat 1 of the eggs and add to the mixture. Stir in with a fork, adding 1–2 tablespoons of cold water to form a stiff dough. Knead lightly on a floured surface and form into a ball.

2   Divide the mixture into 16 pieces and shape into small balls, then flatten to form cakes about 1 cm/¹/₂ inch thick and 7.5 cm/3 inches in diameter. Beat the remaining egg and pour into a shallow dish. Dip the cakes first in a little beaten egg, then in the breadcrumbs until lightly coated.

3   Heat the oil in either a wok or deep-fat fryer to 180°C/350°F and deep-fry the cakes for 2–3 minutes or until golden brown in colour. Using a slotted spoon, remove and drain on absorbent kitchen paper.

4   Meanwhile, blend the hoisin sauce, sugar, 1 tablespoon of water and the sesame oil together until smooth and pour into a small bowl. Serve immediately with the sweetcorn cakes, cucumber and spring onions.

Ingredients   SERVES 6–8

250 g/9 oz self–raising flour
3 tbsp Thai red curry paste
2 tbsp light soy sauce
2 tsp sugar
2 kaffir lime leaves, finely shredded
12 fine French beans, trimmed, finely
   chopped and blanched
340 g can sweetcorn, drained
salt and freshly ground black pepper
2 medium eggs
50 g/2 oz fresh white breadcrumbs
vegetable oil, for deep-frying

For the dipping sauce:

2 tbsp hoisin sauce
1 tbsp soft light brown sugar
1 tbsp sesame oil

To serve:

halved cucumber slices
spring onions, sliced diagonally

Dim Sum Pork Parcels

1 Place the water chestnuts, prawns, pork mince and bacon in a bowl and mix together. Add the soy sauces, Chinese rice wine, ginger, chopped spring onion, sesame oil and egg white. Season to taste with salt and pepper, sprinkle in the sugar and mix the filling thoroughly.

2 Place a spoonful of filling in the centre of a wonton skin. Bring the sides up and press around the filling to make a basket shape. Flatten the base of the skin, so the wonton stands solid. The top should be wide open, exposing the filling.

3 Place the parcels on a heatproof plate, on a wire rack inside a wok or on the base of a muslin-lined bamboo steamer. Place over a wok, half-filled with boiling water, cover, then steam the parcels for about 20 minutes. Do this in two batches.

4 Transfer to a warmed serving plate, sprinkle with toasted sesame seeds, drizzle with soy sauce and serve immediately.

Ingredients   MAKES ABOUT 40

125 g/4 oz canned water chestnuts, drained and finely chopped
125 g/4 oz raw prawns, peeled, de-veined and coarsely chopped
350 g/12 oz fresh pork mince
2 tbsp smoked bacon, finely chopped
1 tbsp light soy sauce, plus extra to serve
1 tsp dark soy sauce
1 tbsp Chinese rice wine
2 tbsp fresh root ginger, peeled and finely chopped
3 spring onions, trimmed and finely chopped
2 tsp sesame oil
1 medium egg white, lightly beaten
salt and freshly ground black pepper
2 tsp sugar
40 wonton skins, thawed if frozen
toasted sesame seeds, to garnish
soy sauce, to serve

Mixed Canapés

1   For the cheese canapés, cut the crusts off the bread, then gently roll with a rolling pin to flatten slightly. Thinly spread with butter, then sprinkle over the mixed cheeses as evenly as possible.

2   Roll up each slice tightly, then cut into four slices, each about 2.5 cm/1 inch long. Heat the oil in a wok or large frying pan and stir-fry the cheese rolls in two batches, turning them all the time until golden brown and crisp. Drain on absorbent kitchen paper and serve warm or cold.

3   For the spicy nuts, melt the butter and oil in a wok, then add the nuts and stir-fry over a low heat for about 5 minutes, stirring all the time, or until they begin to colour.

4   Sprinkle the paprika and cumin over the nuts and continue stir-frying for a further 1–2 minutes, or until the nuts are golden brown.

5   Remove from the wok and drain on absorbent kitchen paper. Sprinkle with the salt, garnish with sprigs of fresh coriander and serve hot or cold. If serving cold, store both the cheese canapés and the spicy nuts in airtight containers.

Ingredients   SERVES 12

For the stir-fried cheese canapés:

6 thick slices white bread
40 g/1^1/$_2$ oz butter, softened
75 g/3 oz mature Cheddar
   cheese, grated
75 g/3 oz blue cheese such as Stilton
   or Gorgonzola, crumbled
3 tbsp sunflower oil

For the spicy nuts:

25 g/1 oz unsalted butter
2 tbsp light olive oil
450 g/1 lb mixed unsalted nuts
1 tsp ground paprika
^{1}/$_2$ tsp ground cumin
^{1}/$_2$ tsp fine sea salt
sprigs of fresh coriander, to garnish

Tasty tip

These canapés are perfect for serving at a buffet or finger food party, or you can halve the quantities and serve with drinks instead of a starter at an informal dinner party for 4–6 people.

Quick Mediterranean Prawns

1 Remove the shells from the prawns, leaving the tail shells. Using a small, sharp knife, remove the dark vein that runs along the back of the prawns. Rinse and drain on absorbent kitchen paper.

2 Whisk 2 tablespoons of the oil with the garlic, lemon zest and juice in a small bowl. Bruise 1 sprig of rosemary with a rolling pin and add to the bowl. Add the prawns, toss to coat, then cover and leave to marinate in the refrigerator until needed.

3 For the simple dips, mix the yogurt and pesto in one bowl and the crème fraîche, tomato paste and mustard in another bowl. Season to taste with salt and pepper.

4 Heat a wok, add the remaining oil and swirl round to coat the sides. Remove the prawns from the marinade, leaving any juices and the rosemary behind. Add to the wok and stir-fry over a high heat for 3–4 minutes, or until the prawns are pink and just cooked through.

5 Remove the prawns from the wok and arrange on a platter. Garnish with lemon wedges and more fresh rosemary sprigs and serve hot or cold with the dips.

Ingredients   SERVES 4

20 raw Mediterranean prawns
3 tbsp olive oil
1 garlic clove, peeled and crushed
juice and finely grated zest
    of $^1/_2$ lemon
sprigs of fresh rosemary

For the pesto & sun-dried tomato dips:

150 ml/$^1/_4$ pint Greek yogurt
1 tbsp prepared pesto
150 ml/$^1/_4$ pint crème fraîche
1 tbsp sun-dried tomato paste
1 tbsp wholegrain mustard
salt and freshly ground black pepper
lemon wedges, to garnish

Tasty tip

The prawns must be cooked thoroughly, but take care not to overcook them or they will be tough. Remove from the refrigerator and leave at room temperature for 15 minutes before stir-frying.

Smoked Haddock Tart

1   Preheat the oven to 190°C/375°F/Gas Mark 5. Sift the flour and salt into a large bowl. Add the fats and mix lightly. Using the fingertips, rub into the flour until the mixture resembles breadcrumbs.

2   Sprinkle 1 tablespoon of cold water into the mixture and, with a knife, start bringing the dough together. It may be necessary to use the hands for the final stage. If the dough does not form a ball instantly, add a little more water. Put the pastry in a polythene bag and chill for at least 30 minutes.

3   On a lightly floured surface, roll out the pastry and use to line an 18 cm/7 inch lightly oiled quiche or flan tin. Prick the base all over with a fork and bake blind in the preheated oven for 15 minutes.

4   Carefully remove the pastry from the oven, brush with a little of the beaten egg.

5   Return to the oven for a further 5 minutes, then place the fish in the pastry case.

6   For the filling, beat together the eggs and cream. Add the mustard, black pepper and cheese and pour over the fish.

7   Sprinkle with the chives and bake for 35–40 minutes or until the filling is golden brown and set in the centre. Serve hot or cold with the lemon and tomato wedges and salad leaves.

Ingredients   SERVES 6

Shortcrust pastry:

150 g/5 oz plain flour
pinch of salt
25 g/1 oz lard or white vegetable fat, cut into small cubes
40 g/1½ oz butter or hard margarine, cut into small cubes

For the filling:

225 g/8 oz smoked haddock, skinned and cubed
2 large eggs, beaten
300 ml/½ pint double cream
1 tsp Dijon mustard
freshly ground black pepper
125 g/4 oz Gruyère cheese, grated
1 tbsp freshly snipped chives

To serve:

lemon wedges
tomato wedges
fresh green salad leaves

2

4

6

Stilton, Tomato & Courgette Quiche

1   Preheat the oven to 190°C/375°F/Gas Mark 5. On a lightly
    floured surface, roll out the pastry and use to line an 18 cm/7
    inch lightly oiled quiche or flan tin, trimming any excess
    pastry with a knife.

2   Prick the base all over with a fork and bake blind in the
    preheated oven for 15 minutes. Remove the pastry from the
    oven and brush with a little of the beaten egg. Return to the
    oven for a further 5 minutes.

3   Heat the butter in a frying pan and gently fry the onion and
    courgette for about 4 minutes until soft and starting to
    brown. Transfer into the pastry case.

4   Sprinkle the Stilton over evenly and top with the halved
    cherry tomatoes. Beat together the eggs and crème fraîche
    and season to taste with salt and pepper.

5   Pour the filling into the pastry case and bake in the oven for
    35–40 minutes, or until the filling is golden brown and set in
    the centre. Serve the quiche hot or cold.

Ingredients   SERVES 4

1 quantity shortcrust pastry (see
    page 190)
25 g/1 oz butter
1 onion, peeled and finely chopped
1 courgette, trimmed and sliced
125 g/4 oz Stilton cheese, crumbled
6 cherry tomatoes, halved
2 large eggs, beaten
200 ml tub crème fraîche
salt and freshly ground black pepper

Food fact

Stilton is a very traditional British
cheese which often makes an
appearance on the cheese board or
served with a ploughman's lunch. It
gets much of its full pungent flavour,
from its veins (created from the steel
wires which are inserted into the
cheese during the maturing process).
It is worth looking for a piece of
Stilton with lots of veins that has been
matured for longer.

1

3

4

French Onion Tart

1 Preheat the oven to 200°C/400°F/Gas Mark 6. Place the butter in the freezer for 30 minutes. Sift the flour and salt into a large bowl. Remove the butter from the freezer and grate using the coarse side of a grater, dipping the butter in the flour every now and again, which will make it easier to grate. Mix the butter into the flour, using a knife, making sure all the butter is coated thoroughly with flour. Add 2 tablespoons of cold water and continue to mix. Use your hands to complete the mixing. Add a little more water if needed, to leave a clean bowl. Place the pastry in a polythene bag and chill in the refrigerator for 30 minutes.

2 Heat the oil in a large frying pan, then fry the onions for 10 minutes, stirring occasionally until softened. Stir in the white wine vinegar and sugar. Increase the heat and stir frequently for another 4–5 minutes until the onions turn a deep caramel colour. Cook for another 5 minutes, then reserve to cool.

3 On a lightly floured surface, roll out the pastry to a 35.5 cm/ 14 inch circle. Wrap over a rolling pin and move the circle on to a baking sheet. Sprinkle half the cheese over the pastry, leaving a 5 cm/2 inch border around the edge, then spoon the caramelised onions over the cheese. Fold the uncovered pastry over the edge of the filling to form a rim and brush it with beaten egg or milk. Season to taste with salt and pepper. Sprinkle over the remaining Cheddar and bake for 20–25 minutes. Transfer to a large plate and serve immediately.

Ingredients SERVES 4

Quick flaky pastry:
125 g/4 oz butter
175 g/6 oz plain flour
pinch of salt

For the filling:
2 tbsp olive oil
4 large onions, peeled and
  thinly sliced
3 tbsp white wine vinegar
2 tbsp muscovado sugar
a little beaten egg or milk
175 g/6 oz Cheddar cheese, grated
salt and freshly ground black pepper

Tasty tip
For a milder, nutty taste, substitute the Cheddar cheese for Gruyère and grate a little nutmeg over the layer of cheese in step 3.

Parsnip Tatin

1 Preheat the oven to 200°C/400°F/Gas Mark 6. Heat the butter in a 20.5 cm/8 inch frying pan.

2 Add the parsnips, arranging the cut side down with the narrow ends towards the centre.

3 Sprinkle the parsnips with sugar and cook for 15 minutes, turning halfway through until golden.

4 Add the apple juice and bring to the boil. Remove the pan from the heat.

5 On a lightly floured surface, roll the pastry out to a size slightly larger than the frying pan.

6 Position the pastry over the parsnips and press down slightly to enclose the parsnips.

7 Bake in the preheated oven for 20–25 minutes until the parsnips and pastry are golden.

8 Invert a warm serving plate over the pan and carefully turn the pan over to flip the tart on to the plate. Serve immediately.

Ingredients   SERVES 4

1 quantity shortcrust pastry
  (see page 190)

For the filling:

50 g/2 oz butter
8 small parsnips, peeled and halved
1 tbsp brown sugar
75 ml/3 fl oz apple juice

Tasty tip

This dish is delicious served warm with a Greek salad. Feta cheese is one of the main ingredients in Greek salad and, because of its salty taste, it is particularly good with the creamy flavour of parsnips in this recipe.

Garlic Wild Mushroom Galettes

1   Preheat the oven to 220˚C/425˚F/Gas Mark 7. On a lightly floured surface, roll out the chilled pastry very thinly.

2   Cut out six 15 cm/6 inch circles and place on a lightly oiled baking sheet.

3   Thinly slice the onion, then divide into rings and reserve.

4   Thinly slice the chilli and slice the garlic into wafer–thin slivers. Add to the onions and reserve.

5   Wipe or lightly rinse the mushrooms. Halve or quarter any large mushrooms and keep the small ones whole.

6   Heat the butter in a frying pan and sauté the onion, chilli and garlic gently for about 3 minutes. Add the mushrooms and cook for about 5 minutes, or until beginning to soften.

7   Stir the parsley into the mushroom mixture and drain off any excess liquid.

8   Pile the mushroom mixture on to the pastry circles within 5 mm/$^1/_4$ inch of the edge. Arrange the sliced mozzarella cheese on top.

9   Bake in the preheated oven for 12–15 minutes, or until golden brown and serve with the tomatoes and salad.

Ingredients   SERVES 6

1 quantity quick flaky pastry (see page 194), chilled
1 onion, peeled
1 red chilli, deseeded
2 garlic cloves, peeled
275 g/10 oz mixed mushrooms e.g. oyster, chestnuts, morels, ceps and chanterelles
25 g/1 oz butter
2 tbsp freshly chopped parsley
125 g/4 oz mozzarella cheese, sliced

To serve:

cherry tomatoes
mixed green salad leaves

Helpful hint

Many supermarkets now stock a variety of wild mushrooms, all of which can be used in this recipe. To maintain their flavour, do not peel them unless they appear old or tough. Either rinse lightly if covered with small pieces of soil or wipe well, trim the stalks and use.

2

5

8

Bacon, Mushroom & Cheese Puffs

1 Preheat the oven to 200°C/400°F/Gas Mark 6. Heat the olive oil in a large frying pan.

2 Add the mushrooms and bacon and fry for 6–8 minutes until golden in colour. Stir in the parsley, season to taste with salt and pepper and allow to cool.

3 Roll the sheet of pastry a little thinner on a lightly floured surface to a 30.5 cm/12 inch square. Cut the pastry into four equal squares.

4 Stir the grated Emmenthal cheese into the mushroom mixture. Spoon a quarter of the mixture on to one half of each square.

5 Brush the edges of the square with a little of the beaten egg.

6 Fold over the pastry to form a triangular parcel. Seal the edges well and place on a lightly oiled baking sheet. Repeat until the squares are done

7 Make shallow slashes in the top of the pastry with a knife.

8 Brush the parcels with the remaining beaten egg and cook in the preheated oven for 20 minutes, or until puffy and golden brown.

9 Serve warm or cold, garnished with the salad leaves and served with tomatoes.

Ingredients   SERVES 4

1 tbsp olive oil
225 g/8 oz field mushrooms, wiped
   and roughly chopped
225 g/8 oz rindless streaky bacon,
   roughly chopped
2 tbsp freshly chopped parsley
salt and freshly ground black pepper
350 g/12 oz ready–rolled puff pastry
   sheets, thawed if frozen
25 g/1 oz Emmenthal cheese, grated
1 medium egg, beaten
salad leaves such as rocket or
   watercress, to garnish
tomatoes, to serve

Tasty tip

The Emmenthal cheese in this recipe can be substituted for any other cheese, but for best results use a cheese such as Cheddar which, like Emmenthal, melts easily. The bacon can also be substituted for slices of sweeter cured hams such as pancetta, speck, Parma or prosciutto.

Fennel & Caramelised Shallot Tartlets

1. Preheat the oven to 200°C/400°F/Gas Mark 6. Sift the flour into a bowl, then rub in the butter, using the fingertips. Stir in the cheese, then add the egg yolk with about 2 tablespoons of cold water. Mix to a firm dough, then knead lightly. Wrap in clingfilm and chill in the refrigerator for 30 minutes.

2. Roll out the pastry on a lightly floured surface and use to line six 10 cm/4 inch individual flan tins or patty tins which are about 2 cm/³/₄ inch deep.

3. Line the pastry cases with greaseproof paper and fill with baking beans or rice. Bake blind in the preheated oven for about 10 minutes, then remove the paper and beans.

4. Heat the oil in a frying pan, add the shallots and fennel and fry gently for 5 minutes. Sprinkle with the sugar and cook for a further 10 minutes, stirring occasionally, until lightly caramelised. Reserve until cooled.

5. Beat together the egg and cream and season to taste with salt and pepper. Divide the shallot mixture between the pastry cases. Pour over the egg mixture and sprinkle with the cheese and cinnamon. Bake for 20 minutes, until golden and set. Serve with the salad leaves.

Ingredients   SERVES 6

Cheese pastry:
175 g/6 oz plain white flour
75 g/3 oz slightly salted butter
50 g/2 oz Gruyère cheese, grated
1 small egg yolk

For the filling:
2 tbsp olive oil
225 g/8 oz shallots, peeled
    and halved
1 fennel bulb, trimmed and sliced
1 tsp soft brown sugar
1 medium egg
150 ml/¹/₄ pint double cream
salt and freshly ground black pepper
25 g/1 oz Gruyère cheese, grated
¹/₂ tsp ground cinnamon
mixed salad leaves, to serve

Smoked Mackerel Vol-au-Vents

1 Preheat the oven to 230°C/450°F/Gas Mark 8. Roll the pastry out on a lightly floured surface and, using a 9 cm/3¹/₂ inch fluted cutter, cut out 12 rounds.

2 Using a 1 cm/¹/₂ inch cutter mark a lid in the centre of each round.

3 Place on a damp baking sheet and brush the rounds with a little beaten egg.

4 Sprinkle the pastry with the sesame seeds and bake in the preheated oven for 10–12 minutes, or until golden brown and well risen.

5 Transfer the vol–au–vents to a chopping board and, when cool enough to touch, carefully remove the lids with a small sharp knife.

6 Scoop out any uncooked pastry from the inside of each vol–au–vent, then return to the oven for 5–8 minutes to dry out. Remove and allow to cool.

7 Flake the mackerel into small pieces and reserve. Peel the cucumber if desired, cut into very small dice and add to the mackerel.

8 Beat the soft cream cheese with the cranberry sauce, dill and lemon rind. Stir in the mackerel and cucumber and use to fill the vol–au–vents. Place the lids on top and garnish with dill sprigs.

Ingredients   MAKES 12

350 g/12 oz prepared puff pastry
1 small egg, beaten
2 tsp sesame seeds
225 g/8 oz peppered smoked
    mackerel, skinned and chopped
5 cm/2 inch piece cucumber
4 tbsp soft cream cheese
2 tbsp cranberry sauce
1 tbsp freshly chopped dill
1 tbsp finely grated lemon rind
dill sprigs, to garnish
mixed salad leaves, to serve

Tasty tip

Mackerel is a relatively cheap fish and one of the richest sources of minerals, oils and vitamins available. This dish is an affordable way to incorporate all these essential nutrients into your diet.

1

5

8

Luxury Fish Pasties

1   Preheat the oven to 200°C/400°F/Gas Mark 6. Place the butter in a saucepan and slowly heat until melted. Add the flour and cook, stirring, for 1 minute. Remove from the heat and gradually add the milk a little at a time, stirring between each addition. Return to the heat and simmer, stirring continuously, until thickened. Remove from the heat and add the salmon, parsley, dill, lime rind, lime juice, prawns and seasoning.

2   Roll out the pastry on a lightly floured surface and cut out six 12.5 cm/5 inch circles and six 15 cm/6 inch circles. Brush the edges of the smallest circle with the beaten egg and place two tablespoons of filling in the centre of each one.

3   Place the larger circle over the filling and press the edges together to seal.

4   Pinch the edge of the pastry between the forefinger and thumb to ensure a firm seal and decorative edge.

5   Cut a slit in each parcel, brush with the beaten egg and sprinkle with sea salt.

6   Transfer to a baking sheet and cook in the preheated oven for 20 minutes, or until golden brown. Serve immediately with some fresh green salad leaves.

Ingredients   SERVES 6

2 quantities of quick flaky pastry (see page 194), chilled
125 g/4 oz butter
125 g/4oz plain flour
300 ml/$^1/_2$ pint milk
225 g/8 oz salmon fillet, skinned and cut into chunks
1 tbsp freshly chopped parsley
1 tbsp freshly chopped dill
juice and grated rind of 1 lime
225 g/8 oz peeled prawns
salt and freshly ground black pepper
1 small egg, beaten
1 tsp sea salt
fresh green salad leaves, to serve

Helpful hint

Salmon is not only full of minerals but is a vital source of calcium, as well as being extremely low in fat. Ensure when using raw prawns that the vein that runs along the back of the prawn is removed.

Olive & Feta Parcels

1   Preheat the oven to 180°C/350°F/Gas Mark 4. Preheat the grill, then line the grill rack with foil.

2   Cut the peppers into quarters and remove the seeds. Place skin-side up on the foil-lined grill rack and cook under the preheated grill for 10 minutes, turning occasionally, until the skins begin to blacken. Place the peppers in a polythene bag and leave until cool enough to handle, then skin and thinly slice.

3   Chop the olives and cut the feta cheese into small cubes. Mix together the olives, feta, sliced peppers and pine nuts.

4   Cut 1 sheet of filo pastry in half then brush with a little of the oil. Place a spoonful of the olive and feta mix about one-third of the way up the pastry. Fold over the pastry and wrap to form a square parcel encasing the filling completely.

5   Place this parcel in the centre of the second half of the pastry sheet. Brush the edges lightly with a little oil, bring up the corners to meet in the centre and twist them loosely to form a purse. Brush with a little more oil and repeat with the remaining filo pastry and filling.

6   Place the parcels on a lightly oiled baking sheet and bake in the preheated oven for 10–15 minutes, or until crisp and golden brown. Serve with the dip.

Ingredients   MAKES 30

1 small red pepper
1 small yellow pepper
125 g/4 oz assorted marinated green and black olives
125 g/4 oz feta cheese
2 tbsp pine nuts, lightly toasted
6 sheets filo pastry
3 tbsp olive oil
soured cream and chive dip, to serve

Helpful hint

Feta is generally made from goats' milk and has quite a salty taste. To make the cheese less salty simply soak it in milk, then drain before eating.

2

4

5

Antipasti with Focaccia

1 Preheat oven to 220°C/425°F/Gas Mark 7, 15 minutes before baking. Arrange the fresh fruit, vegetables, prawns, sardines, olives, cheese and meat on a large serving platter. Drizzle over 1 tablespoon of the olive oil, then cover and chill in the refrigerator while making the bread.

2 Sift the flour, sugar, semolina and salt into a large mixing bowl then sprinkle in the dried yeast. Make a well in the centre and add the remaining 2 tablespoons of olive oil. Add the warm water, a little at a time, and mix together until a smooth, pliable dough is formed. If using fresh yeast, cream the yeast with the sugar, then gradually beat in half the warm water. Leave in a warm place until frothy then proceed as for dried yeast.

3 Place on to a lightly floured board and knead until smooth and elastic. Place the dough in a lightly greased bowl, cover and leave in a warm place for 45 minutes.

4 Knead again and flatten the dough into a large, flat oval shape about 1 cm/¹/₂ inch thick. Place on a lightly oiled baking tray. Prick the surface with the end of a wooden spoon and brush with olive oil. Sprinkle on the coarse salt and bake in the preheated oven for 25 minutes, or until golden. Serve the bread with the prepared platter of food.

Ingredients   SERVES 4

3 fresh figs, quartered
125 g/4 oz green beans, cooked
   and halved
1 small head of radicchio, rinsed
   and shredded
125 g/4 oz large prawns, peeled
   and cooked
125 can sardines, drained
25 g/1 oz pitted black olives
25 g/1 oz stuffed green olives
125 g/4 oz mozzarella cheese, sliced
50 g/2 oz Italian salami sausage,
   thinly sliced
3 tbsp olive oil

For the focaccia:

275 g/10 oz strong white flour
pinch of sugar
3 tsp easy–blend quick–acting yeast
   or 15 g/¹/₂ oz fresh yeast
175 g/6 oz fine semolina
1 tsp salt
300 ml/¹/₂ pint warm water
a little extra olive oil for brushing
1 tbsp coarse salt crystals

1

2

3

Mozzarella Frittata with Tomato & Basil Salad

1 To make the tomato and basil salad, slice the tomatoes very thinly, tear up the basil leaves and sprinkle over. Make the dressing by whisking the olive oil, lemon juice and sugar together well. Season with black pepper before drizzling the dressing over the salad.

2 To make the frittata, preheat the grill to a high heat, just before beginning to cook. Place the eggs in a large bowl with plenty of salt and whisk. Grate the mozzarella and stir into the egg with the finely chopped spring onions.

3 Heat the oil in a large, non-stick frying pan and pour in the egg mixture, stirring with a wooden spoon to spread the ingredients evenly over the pan.

4 Cook for 5–8 minutes, until the frittata is golden brown and firm on the underside. Place the whole pan under the preheated grill and cook for about 4–5 minutes, or until the top is golden brown. Slide the frittata on to a serving plate, cut into six large wedges and serve immediately with the tomato and basil salad and plenty of warm crusty bread.

Ingredients   SERVES 6

For the salad:

6 ripe but firm tomatoes
2 tbsp fresh basil leaves
2 tbsp olive oil
1 tbsp fresh lemon juice
1 tsp caster sugar
freshly ground black pepper

For the frittata:

7 medium eggs, beaten
salt
300 g/11 oz mozzarella cheese
2 spring onions, trimmed and
    finely chopped
2 tbsp olive oil
warm crusty bread, to serve

Fried Whitebait with Rocket Salad

1 If the whitebait are frozen, thaw completely, then wipe dry with absorbent kitchen paper.

2 Start to heat the oil in a deep-fat fryer. Arrange the fish in a large, shallow dish and toss well in the flour, cayenne pepper and salt and pepper.

3 Deep-fry the fish in batches for 2–3 minutes, or until crisp and golden. Keep the cooked fish warm while deep-frying the remaining fish.

4 Meanwhile, to make the salad, arrange the rocket leaves, cherry tomatoes and cucumber on individual serving dishes. Whisk the olive oil and the remaining ingredients together and season lightly. Drizzle the dressing over the salad and serve with the whitebait.

Ingredients SERVES 4

450 g/1 lb whitebait, fresh or frozen
oil, for frying
85 g/3 oz plain flour
$\frac{1}{2}$ tsp cayenne pepper
salt and freshly ground black pepper

For the salad:

125 g/4 oz rocket leaves
125 g/4 oz cherry tomatoes, halved
75 g/3 oz cucumber, cut into dice
3 tbsp olive oil
1 tbsp fresh lemon juice
$\frac{1}{2}$ tsp Dijon mustard
$\frac{1}{2}$ tsp caster sugar

Tasty tip

Why not try a different salad? Mix together some cleaned baby spinach, cooled, cooked petits pois and chopped spring onions, then pour over 2 tablespoons of garlic olive oil. If serving with a chicken dish, top the salad with some feta cheese.

Bruschetta with Pecorino, Garlic & Tomatoes

1 Preheat the grill and line the grill rack with foil just before cooking. Make a small cross in the top of the tomatoes, then place in a small bowl and cover with boiling water. Leave to stand for 2 minutes, then drain and remove the skins. Cut into quarters, remove the seeds, and chop the flesh into small dice.

2 Mix the tomato flesh with the pecorino cheese and 2 teaspoons of the fresh oregano and season to taste with salt and pepper. Add 1 tablespoon of the olive oil and mix thoroughly.

3 Crush the garlic and spread evenly over the slices of bread. Heat 2 tablespoons of the olive oil in a large frying pan and sauté the bread slices until they are crisp and golden.

4 Place the fried bread on a lightly oiled baking tray and spoon on the tomato and cheese topping. Place a little mozzarella on top and place under the preheated grill for 3–4 minutes, until golden and bubbling. Garnish with the remaining oregano, then arrange the bruschettas on a serving plate and serve immediately with the olives.

Ingredients   SERVES 4

6 ripe but firm tomatoes
125 g/4 oz pecorino cheese,
   finely grated
1 tbsp oregano leaves
salt and freshly ground black pepper
3 tbsp olive oil
3 garlic cloves, peeled
8 slices of flat Italian bread, such
   as focaccia
50 g/2 oz mozzarella cheese
marinated black olives, to serve

Tasty tip

Bitter leaves are excellent with these bruschettas because they help to offset the richness of the cheese and tomato topping. Try a mixture of frisée, radicchio and rocket. If these are unavailable, use a bag of mixed salad leaves.

Crostini with Chicken Livers

1 Heat 1 tablespoon of the olive oil and 1 tablespoon of the butter in a frying pan, add the shallot and garlic and cook gently for 2–3 minutes.

2 Trim and wash the chicken livers thoroughly and pat dry on absorbent kitchen paper as much as possible. Cut into slices, then toss in the flour. Add the livers to the frying pan with the shallot and garlic and continue to fry for a further 2 minutes, stirring continuously.

3 Pour in the white wine and brandy and bring to the boil. Boil rapidly for 1–2 minutes to allow the alcohol to evaporate, then stir in the sliced mushrooms and cook gently for about 5 minutes, or until the chicken livers are cooked, but just a little pink inside. Season to taste with salt and pepper.

4 Fry the slices of ciabatta or similar–style bread in the remaining oil and butter, then place on individual serving dishes. Spoon over the liver mixture and garnish with a few sage leaves and lemon wedges. Serve immediately.

Ingredients   SERVES 4

2 tbsp olive oil
2 tbsp butter
1 shallot, peeled and finely chopped
1 garlic clove, peeled and crushed
150 g/5 oz chicken livers
1 tbsp plain flour
2 tbsp dry white wine
1 tbsp brandy
50 g/2 oz mushrooms, sliced
salt and freshly ground black pepper
4 slices of ciabatta or similar bread

To garnish:

fresh sage leaves
lemon wedges

Tasty tip

If you prefer a lower fat alternative to the fried bread in this recipe, omit 1 tablespoon of the butter and brush the bread slices with the remaining 1 tablespoon of oil. Bake in a preheated oven at 180°C/350°F/Gas Mark 4 for about 20 minutes, or until golden and crisp, then serve as above.

Italian Baked Tomatoes with Curly Endive & Radicchio

1 Preheat the oven to 190°C/375°F/Gas Mark 5. Lightly oil a baking tray with the teaspoon of oil. Slice the tops off the tomatoes and remove all the tomato flesh and sieve into a large bowl. Sprinkle a little salt inside the tomato shells and then place them upside down on a plate while the filling is prepared.

2 Mix the sieved tomato with the breadcrumbs, fresh herbs and mushrooms and season well with salt and pepper. Place the tomato shells on the prepared baking tray and fill with the tomato and mushroom mixture. Sprinkle the cheese on the top and bake in the preheated oven for 15–20 minutes, until golden brown.

3 Meanwhile, prepare the salad. Arrange the endive and radicchio on individual serving plates and mix the remaining ingredients together in a small bowl to make the dressing. Season to taste.

4 When the tomatoes are cooked, allow to rest for 5 minutes, then place on the prepared plates and drizzle over a little dressing. Serve warm.

Ingredients   SERVES 4

1 tsp olive oil
4 beef tomatoes
salt
50 g/2 oz fresh white breadcrumbs
1 tbsp freshly snipped chives
1 tbsp freshly chopped parsley
125 g/4 oz button mushrooms,
    finely chopped
salt and freshly ground black pepper
25 g/1 oz fresh Parmesan
    cheese, grated

For the salad:

$^{1}/_{2}$ curly endive lettuce
$^{1}/_{2}$ small piece of radicchio
2 tbsp olive oil
1 tsp balsamic vinegar
salt and freshly ground black pepper

Spaghettini with Lemon Pesto & Cheese & Herb Bread

1 Preheat the oven to 200°C/400°F/Gas Mark 6, 15 minutes before baking. Mix together the onion, oregano, parsley, butter and cheese. Spread the bread with the cheese mixture, place on a lightly oiled baking tray and cover with foil. Bake in the preheated oven for 10–15 minutes, then keep warm.

2 Add the spaghettini with 1 tablespoon of olive oil to a large saucepan of fast–boiling, lightly salted water and cook for 3–4 minutes, or until 'al dente'. Drain, reserving 2 tablespoons of the cooking liquor.

3 Blend the basil, pine nuts, garlic, Parmesan cheese, lemon rind and juice and remaining olive oil in a food processor or blender until a purée is formed. Season to taste with salt and pepper, then place in a saucepan.

4 Heat the lemon pesto very gently until piping hot, then stir in the pasta together with the reserved cooking liquor. Add the butter and mix together well.

5 Add plenty of black pepper to the pasta and serve immediately with the warm cheese and herb bread.

Ingredients SERVES 4

1 small onion, peeled and grated
2 tsp freshly chopped oregano
1 tbsp freshly chopped parsley
75 g/3 oz butter
125 g/4 oz pecorino cheese, grated
8 slices of Italian flat bread
275 g/10 oz dried spaghettini
4 tbsp olive oil
1 large bunch basil, approximately
    25 g/1 oz
75 g/3 oz pine nuts
1 garlic clove, peeled and crushed
75 g/3 oz Parmesan cheese, grated
juice and finely grated rind
    of 2 lemons
salt and freshly ground black pepper
4 tsp butter

Index